RETHINK YOUR RETIREMENT

Unconventional Wisdom for Safer Retirement Planning

RETHINK YOUR RETIREMENT

*Un*conventional Wisdom for
Safer Retirement Planning

Nathan R. Frederico

CAZADOR PRESS
2019

First Printing: 2019

ISBN 978-1-387-67970-6

Frederico, Nathan R.

Rethink your retirement: Unconventional wisdom for safer retirement planning

Printed in the United States

www.rethinkretirementbook.com

To Jed Mayfield, my mentor and friend.

Contents

Acknowledgements

In my writing process, I've been inspired by revolutionary, innovative thinkers. What motivated them to rethink everyday practices in their own lives?

I read a quote that struck me from Sir Isaac Newton, whose rethinking was allegedly and famously kicked off by an apple hitting him on the head: "If I have seen further than others, it is by standing upon the shoulders of giants."

I have several giants of my own to thank, most notably the man with a giant heart, William Jed Mayfield, who introduced me to a safer world of retirement planning. I strive to honor him and carry on his important work of providing priceless peace of mind to retirees.

Thank you to all who helped me with the writing of this book, including Bill Broich, Tom Bradley, David Townsend, and Anthony Owen for their generosity in being my sounding board as I pinged idea after idea until one would stick. Thank you for believing in me and my vision.

I also owe a debt of gratitude to my wife, Krista, for her time editing each draft, and our two sons for their love and enthusiasm. Special thanks to my parents and my wife's parents for their valuable feedback on early versions of this book, and for sharing what these ideas meant to them as retirees.

Introduction

"I have a solution, but you're not going to like it."

I vividly remember my first meeting with Gladys, an 82-year-old avid hiker who loves desert gardening. Her husband, who had passed away four years earlier, worked as an electrician, and they raised a wonderful family while enjoying a comfortable life in Tucson, Arizona.

First meetings are usually upbeat, and just involve light conversation about the individual's past, present, and goals for the future. But in this meeting, Gladys interrupted the pleasantries with a pressing concern: she needed a second opinion on her financial accounts right away. The paperwork was complicated and she was unsure about what it all meant. I looked at her stack of recent financial statements and immediately, I was worried. Lively, engaging Gladys had hardly any money left in her retirement savings. Unless something changed, her money wouldn't last another year.

I wish I could tell you that Gladys' predicament was simply a misunderstanding, like she hoped.

I wish I could say Gladys' situation was unique.

Unfortunately, *longevity risk*, or a situation where a retiree's life lasts longer than their money, is more common today than ever in the history of American retirement. While some seniors can lean on family support, others are forced into bankruptcy. The percent of seniors aged 65-74 filing bankruptcy *quintupled* from 1991 to 2016, according to Consumer Bankruptcy Project data, going from a modest 2.1 percent to a staggering 12 percent of all bankruptcy filers.[1] This is typically the age of early retirement: enjoying golf, travel, and other leisure activities that weren't possible during the workweek. Now seniors are an increasingly economically vulnerable age group, living their "golden years fraught with economic risk," according to the study. What happened?

For Gladys, some may say her trouble began when she was in her early 70s during the stock market crash of 2008. But truthfully, her financial crisis started back when she and her husband first retired in the early 2000s and did not adequately protect their retirement.

After the stock market crash, Gladys and her husband moved their investment funds out of the market, selling their holdings and essentially locking in their losses. Most would call this an error, but I see it as simply human nature: in a crisis, we protect ourselves. But where was that urge to protect themselves earlier? They certainly did not think they were acting irresponsibly. They thought—and were told by their prior financial advisor—that Wall Street was the best place for all their money, until it wasn't.

As I thought about this situation, I couldn't help but wonder, "What led this couple to believe the stock market was suitable for all their hard-earned retirement savings?"

- Was it optimism in the U.S. stock market's potential?
- Was it reckless greed? My mentor Jed Mayfield always said, "Greedy keeps you needy," which seemed to describe Gladys' current state.

But those answers didn't sit right. The more I considered it, the more I realized that in a world of conflicting information, it is easy to be confused on how to prepare for retirement. And whether due to misunderstandings or misplaced expectations, many have lost their retirement futures. We can't change the past, but we can honor it by learning from it. We can *educate ourselves* and avoid putting all *your* hard-earned life savings at risk, and that is the focus of this book.

Why the need to Rethink Your Retirement?

Clearly, we have an escalating national retirement crisis on our hands. Costs of living, especially for healthcare, are steadily *increasing*, pensions are steadily *declining*, and at times, Wall Street is *just plain unsteady*. In these uncertain times, I subscribe to a statement attributed to Albert Einstein: "We cannot solve problems using the same kind of thinking as we did when we created them."

And what is that kind of thinking that brought us here? In retirement, I've found that even though each person's financial situation is unique, many retirees tend to approach retirement planning in the same way: leaving almost all their retirement savings at risk in Wall Street's control. That practice allows for too much uncertainty—and **in retirement, you need fewer uncertainties and more *guarantees*. There are safer ways to plan that will provide the stability, security, and peace of mind that you deserve.**

Now, it remains true that Wall Street can be a useful vehicle for growth. And it seems rational to leave your money where it has historically performed well. But the stock market also involves serious risks, especially for those nearing retirement. Arguably, the stock market has never been more volatile, more manipulated, or had more of our retirement money under its control. How much of your well-being is left to chance?

Don't Leave Money on the Table

Superior financial tools can reduce or even eliminate risk in retirement. But they're not as well known. Why? These strategies tend to decrease retirees' dependence on the stock market, and Wall Street brokers don't want that. They spend big advertising dollars to persuade retirees that Wall Street is the best option for all their savings. Most financial advisors affiliate with one of these big brokers and predictably tailor their retirement advice to fit their firm's Wall Street services.

What happens when advisors or firms sidestep reliable solutions, and consumers aren't aware of what to ask for? Unfortunately, retirees may leave better opportunities—and money—on the table.

If there's ever a time for comprehensive financial planning, it should be when you are preparing to take the retirement leap. **Just as you likely spent years in college or vocational training to prepare for the next few decades of your career, it makes sense to educate yourself and thoroughly prepare for the next few decades you will spend in retirement.** And you shouldn't feel alone in this process. Find your own trusted retirement planner, one who is willing to use any worthy financial tools to your advantage.

For Gladys, that financial tool was something she never expected. I recognized in reviewing her account that while Gladys had nearly depleted her finances, she lived in a fully paid-off home. I didn't sugar coat it: I told her that her retirement funds were unsustainably low, but there was a way forward. Shocked but determined, we planned together for her to take a reverse mortgage and budget her remaining money for lifetime retirement income. Today, she is proud that she navigated her financial trouble and put her retirement back on course.

An Overview

This book is primarily written for those fast-approaching retirement or perhaps already there. It has no new inventions; in fact, you may have heard some of these ideas before. But it was literary genius Mark Twain who said, "There is no such thing as a new idea. It is impossible. We simply take a lot of old ideas and put them into a sort of mental kaleidoscope. We give them a turn and they make new and curious combinations."[2]

In that spirit, the following chapters discuss tried-and-true financial products in plain language, getting rid of myths and double-talk. Hopefully, it will spark reconsideration or a rethink of how certain products working together could be ideal for your retirement plan.

Chapter 1 gives an overview of pensions and their increasingly dominant replacement, the 401(k). Knowing more about both these retirement savings plans, including their benefits and drawbacks, can help you better evaluate how you are saving for retirement.

Can you spot a safe investment when you see one? In **Chapter 2**, which explains the basics of portfolio diversification or Modern Portfolio Theory, I offer a helpful rubric to evaluate if you have a safeguarded portion of your retirement savings.

In **Chapter 3**, school is in session, and I'm teaching a course on the misunderstood, misrepresented, and even misused fixed annuity. Is it what you think it is?

Chapter 4 looks at a long-term relationship: our American relationship with risk. It's celebrated in action movies and on Wall Street, where we're told again and again that you take risks to receive rewards. Is this true when it comes to the money you need in retirement?

Do you have a "retirement number"? **Chapter 5** explores the fad of having a singular number that you're aiming to save, and examines why that might be adding anxiety without providing security. By switching your thinking from "what can I save?" to "what can I obtain with what I've saved?" you can find yourself better equipped to maintain your current lifestyle without worrying about a dwindling pile of money.

I don't hold back in these chapters on calling out the issues I have seen in my career, which began as a Wall Street money manager for nearly a decade before a series of events, including the Great Recession, caused me to rethink my clients' complete reliance on risk and chance. I tried on my own to deescalate their exposure to market forces, to meet with clients to assess risk tolerance and rebalance portfolios, but I hit internal brick walls as I tried to rethink this process from within a Wall Street firm. Just as I stepped back, I met Jed Mayfield, a 25-year veteran retirement planner and host of the *Worry-Free Financial Solutions* radio show in Tucson, Arizona. His vision for safer retirement planning met the needs of thousands of Southern Arizonans, as well as addressed some of my concerns about reliance on Wall Street alone as a one-size-fits-all retirement solution.

Under his mentorship, I joined Mayfield Financial and later became accredited as a Retirement Income Certified Professional ®, which opened my eyes to *all* the ways (not just the Wall Street-approved ways) to help clients plan for retirement. My clients and I have the same goals in mind: reduced risk, steady growth, and lasting income. With this type of financial planning, retirees prepare for retirement and beyond with less stress and more success.

This book offers ways for you to reconsider the current conventional wisdom in retirement planning and weigh the available alternatives. These are ways to think differently, to reevaluate myths and misunderstanding, to challenge the taken-for-granted. I believe this kind of rethinking will drive progress in the retirement planning field. Steve Jobs, one of the visionary thinkers of our era, led a 1997 advertisement campaign for Apple with these words:

> "Here's to the crazy ones... The ones who see things differently. They're not fond of rules, and they have no respect for the status quo. You can quote them, disagree with them, glorify and vilify them. About the only thing you can't do is ignore them because they change things. They push the human race forward."

I say here's to you, your future, and your potential to retire on your terms. I hope that you will take this general information, make notes, but most of all, ask questions as you read. Please feel free to submit your questions on my website or through email. And, for those who can, I invite you to bring your questions and meet with me personally to discuss how you can regain control of your money, reimagine your financial potential, and rethink your retirement.

Chapter 1:
No Pension, No Problem

Main Ideas:

- **Your parents' generation may have said, "Retirement planning? What's that for? We just have our pension!"**
- **Pensions' safe lifetime income options for retired workers are on the decline in preference to 401(k)s, a very different way of planning for retirement that gives retirees more responsibility—and risk.**
- **What can you do to keep pace with this major generational shift in American retirement?**

Imagine you're witnessing a celebration in a professional baseball team's clubhouse, complete with cheers and flowing champagne. Take a guess: what do you think is the reason for the party? Perhaps a playoff victory? Maybe a walk-off win in the bottom of the ninth? Actually, it could be a completely different kind of win. Clubhouses also celebrate veteran players' ten-year anniversaries of being in the big leagues. Of all the milestones, why the hoopla for this one? Because the ten-year mark secures a highly sought-after career achievement: a fully vested Major League Baseball lifetime pension.

"It's a goal of everybody that comes into the game... get your ten years and ride off in[to] the sunset," explained Philadelphia Phillies pitcher Tommy Hunter.[3] It's a rare achievement these days to have ten years in the league with the possibility of career-ending injuries and teams opting for younger and younger players each year. And the draw, a minimum of $68,000 a year for life, is significant even for players with multi-million dollar contracts. That might make you scratch your head and ask, "Really? These millionaire superstars are excited about *pensions*? Why?"

Pensions: Mailbox Money and the Three Legged Stool

Pensions have a few misconceptions, so let's make sure we are all on the same page. A pension is a periodic payment to an individual that typically begins in retirement. It is commonly called "mailbox money" because of how it tends to arrive in the mail as a monthly check. There are two types of pensions: 1) public, for example, Social Security; and 2) private, from companies. In this chapter, I'll be talking about private pensions, also called a *Defined Benefit Plan*. These Defined Benefit Plan payments are usually tied to years of service, leading to the name "golden handcuffs," as the employee has a strong financial incentive to remain loyal to the same employer until retirement. Harsh imagery aside, the promise for employees was that if they had a long career for the same organization, they could enjoy a safe and reliable income for life. And retaining employees and promoting productivity would be good for the employer. A win-win, right?

Unfortunately, some pensions have had their problems. In newsworthy circumstances, they have been overpromised and underfunded, making for costly organizational overhead that hurts profitability. Today, private pensions are at a 35-year low and the trend keeps heading down. At one point, 88 percent of workers who had a workplace retirement plan had a pension. Now, only 18 percent of private-sector workers have pension coverage. But the motive behind pensions, that individuals ought to have a steady stream of income in retirement, is an alluring goal, even for those million-dollar contract-earning professional athletes.

The happiest people in retirement tend to be those with a private pension, stated a 2003 University of Michigan study.[4] Does this mean other retirees are doomed?

In your parents' generation, U.S. retirement was commonly characterized as a three-legged stool, supported by Social Security, self-funded savings, and an *employer pension*. Now while pensions have never been perfect, the fact is that they offered many retirees dependable money for life and complemented the other sources of retirement income. It goes without saying that if that latter leg of the stool is missing, the entire retirement will be unstable. Without pensions, you and your generation have to prepare for retirement differently than generations past, and this requires a shift—or a rethink—about retirement planning.

Living Longer, Saving Less

In my experience as a financial advisor, I have found that many Americans have yet to make this shift in their thinking. Others are sounding the alarm: in 2014, the Stanford Center on Longevity found that nearly one-third of Baby Boomers had **no money saved** in retirement plans in 2014, when they were on average 58 years old.[5] The Economic Policy Institute found that for those approaching retirement (between ages 55-64) with positive savings balances, the median account value was just $120,000.[6] This is not enough for the long life expectancies we expect for this generation, especially without a steady private pension.

What does this mean for you, your hard-earned money, and your quality of life in retirement? To answer these questions, it is important to recognize

WAR DEPARTMENT.

REVOLUTIONARY CLAIM.

I CERTIFY That, in conformity with the Law of the United States, of the 18th of March, 1818, *Alijah Hubbard* late a *Sergeant* in the Army of the Revolution, is inscribed on the Pension List, Roll of the *New York* Agency, at the rate of *eight* dollars per month, to commence on the *thirteenth* day of *April* one thousand eight hundred and eighteen.

GIVEN at the War Office of the United States, this *seventeenth* day of *November* one thousand eight hundred and *eighteen.*

J. C. Calhoun

Secretary of War.

1818 United States Revolutionary War Pension Claim. Source: U.S. National Archives.

your generation's unique place in the history of American retirement.

History of Pensions

Pensions have a rich tradition in America, as old as America itself. In 1776, during the Revolutionary War, the Continental Congress agreed that all Revolutionary disabled war veterans would receive a regular half-pay income for life as a reward for their service.[7]

Even further into history, in Ancient Rome, Emperor Augustus rose to power and built the enormous Roman empire with the help of a large and loyal private army. Why were they loyal? Because he had promised them very generous pensions: for 16 years of service, he would give them a pension of 12 times their annual salary.[8]

However, the Emperor underestimated the enormity of this expense. Despite Ancient Rome's vast tax base in the expansive Roman empire, pensions took half of all tax revenues. In fact, some economists attribute Rome's fall partly to its inability to pay out pensions.

It seems that those that fail to learn from history are doomed to repeat it, and pension pay-out issues continue today. Some pensions are not paying for themselves like employers hoped. In Defined Benefit Pension plans, employers invest money in the pension fund for their employees, estimating that by the time the employees retire, this managed pension fund will have enough to make agreed-upon payments for the rest of that person's life. However, this has not always been the case. The 2008 financial crisis pummeled pension funds with devastating losses. Even by 2016, with a strong stock market recovery, many pensions funds remained underfunded.

Against the backdrop of these pension problems, employers began to rethink their retirement plan offerings in the 1980s, leading to a major shift in retirement planning that our society is still getting accustomed to today. Enter the 401(k).

Good Thinking: 401(k) Plans

Who? Some companies offer a 401(k), or a retirement savings plan, for employees that include specific investment options.

What? They can also be called a 401(a), 403(b), or 457 plan based on the tax structure of the business or non-profit with the plan.

Where? Typically, money comes from employees' paycheck by election, with some companies offering a certain matched contribution into their employees' plans as a workplace benefit.

Why? Tax deferral. This money is deposited into the account pre-tax, meaning no taxes *yet* on either the contribution amount or what your employer put in. Employers also receive certain tax advantages for matching the funds.

How? A 401(k) plan can be managed by a financial advisor or advisement firm, acting as investment managers.

When? You can usually only access 401(k) funds when you retire, reach the age of 59 ½, leave your job, or experience a hardship or disability. If you need the funds outside of one of these situations, be prepared to pay penalties.

What about 401(a), 403(b) and 457 plans? These are plans for non-profit entities that essentially work the same as the 401(k) plan.

401(k)s: From Defined Benefit to Defined Contribution

For many, 401(k) plans are the modern replacement to pensions. They allow employees to contribute pre-tax employment income, called "elective deferral," to a fund held for the employee, and employers can choose to match those funds. These are Defined *Contribution* Plans, in contrast to their Defined *Benefit* Plan pension counterparts. They were originally simply a tax avoidance tactic for profit-sharing plans. The uncreative name comes from placement in section 401(k) of the Revenue Act of 1978.

"401(k)s were never designed as the nation's primary retirement system," said Anthony Webb, a research economist at the Center for Retirement Research. "They came to be that as a historical accident."[9]

Accident or not, businesses quickly grew fond of the opportunities a 401(k) presented, and they gained traction. In 1985, there were only 30,000 401(k) plans, while pension plans numbered around 170,000. Around that time, President Ronald Reagan offered his support for pension continuity, stating, **"The private pension system will continue to play a prominent role in ensuring that all Americans have good choices in planning for their retirement years."**[10]

But, Reagan didn't predict that as the 401(k) plan rose in popularity throughout the next decades, it ended up dominating pensions. By 2005, only 20 years later, the statistics were nearly the opposite from before: just 41,000 pension, or Defined Benefit Plans and a staggering 417,000 Defined Contribution, or 401(k) plans.

Figure 1
Private-Sector Workers Participating in Employment-Based
Retirement Plans, by Plan Type, 1979–2014
(Among All Workers)

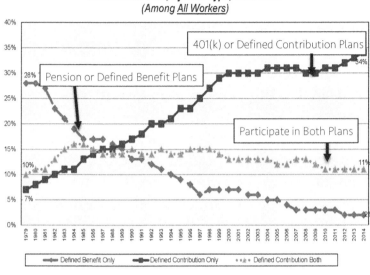

Source: U.S. Department of Labor Form 5500 Summaries 1979-1998, Pension Benefit Guaranty Corporation,
Current Population Survey 1999-2013, EBRI estimates 1999-2014.

401(k) plans do offer serious advantages for businesses and employees. One benefit is that the "golden handcuffs" are essentially removed. After satisfying vesting schedules, 401(k) plans can be transferred from employer to employer, giving individuals opportunities to maintain those pre-tax savings while still making career moves.

Another lesser-known benefit is that as you near retirement, **most 401(k) plans allow you to withdraw your money at age 59.5 so that you can carry out your own retirement planning strategies.** This puts you in the driver's seat, a level of control that those with pensions do not have.

Advantages aside, the fact is that while pensions have a long history for us to learn from, the 401(k) is comparatively new and unproven. The U.S. has yet to have an entire generation of workers begin with, retire with, and subsist on 401(k)s—with no pensions. And yet, **this untested method will soon be used by the largest generation of upcoming retirees in American history!** Even the champions of the 401(k) admit that it has fallen far short of their expectations. Given bankruptcy concerns from earlier in the book, to say that the stakes are high would be an understatement. What are the causes for concern that retirees should be thinking—and rethinking—about?

Issue #1: Only the Lucky Ones

Only about half of American businesses offer a 401(k) plan. According to Pew Charitable Trust research, 53% of small- to mid-sized businesses, or those with 5 - 250 employees, offer this retirement plan.[11] Some of the hesitance is fees, fees, and more fees: many plans require set-up fees, annual fees, advisory fees, plus fees per employee participating. Also, small businesses may not offer 401(k) plans because they think they are required to match employee contributions. This isn't true: small businesses can offer employees the 401(k) tax-deferral benefits without matching those funds.

Costs, misunderstandings, and complications all pose **barriers to offering employees a 401(k) plan,** which is tough for employees who need to maximize these savings tools throughout their working years.

Issue #2: When Your Best Isn't Enough

Another problem is that some employees with 401(k)s are **not contributing enough**. A Vanguard report found that for employees aged 45-54 and preparing for retirement, the median 401(k) savings was only $43,467.[12] Especially given that in 2018, the allowable annual contribution was up to $18,500, with workers over 50 able to contribute $6,000 more, a 401(k) account of less than $45,000 total is lower than it ought to be for this age group. Most Americans are simply saving less for retirement than they could and should be...

Issue #3: Letting Employers Off the Hook

...And since defined contributions are often matched-fund plans, when **employees don't contribute, employers don't either.** One study found that when companies switched to 401(k) plans from pensions, the amount they contributed on behalf of each employee was *cut almost in half.*[13] American workers are letting their employers off the hook.

Issue #4: You Don't Know What You Don't Know

Lack of consumer information poses another serious problem—especially if someone unknowingly ends up in a plan with the wrong amount of risk. How would that happen? Most 401(k) **plans are incredibly complicated for participants**. Anyone who has ever looked over their workplace's plan can attest to the long and confusing list of mutual fund options. It seems like you need a degree in finance just to make sense of it. Plus, it's hard to know much about the nature of the fund just by looking at their names, like "Voyager," "Enterprise," and "New Horizons." It sounds like a space science fiction movie title! Sure, employers may provide opportunities to meet with their 401(k) provider to discuss options, but these meetings often aren't personalized and don't include a comprehensive suitability assessment.

Ted Benna, the consultant who first noticed the obscure line of the 1978 tax code, giving him the title "The Father of the 401(k)," has argued that typical plans offer far too many choices, saying "I am not convinced we have added value by getting more complicated. **If I were starting over from scratch today with what we know, I'd blow up the existing structure and start over.**"[14] Sounds like the inventor laments creating the Frankenstein monster!

Issue #5: The Wall Street Takeover

Before the shift to 401(k)s, employee pension plans were typically managed in conservative strategies to help assure the promised return in two or three decades when that employee retired. Pension managers primarily steered clear of the risks of Wall Street, limiting the funds to low- to no-risk options, like U.S. Treasury Bonds. But 401(k)s are Wall Street funds. Low risk options still involve risk. While employees may be more vulnerable, Wall Street is more dominant than ever.

Ted Benna, reflecting on the 401(k) machine he built, said he regrets he **"helped open the door for Wall Street to make even more money than they were already making."**[15] And at whose expense?

It All Comes Down to You

What's the common denominator in all of these issues? A shift to *you,* and your responsibilities in preparing for retirement. Remember the three-legged stool analogy? If the pension leg is missing, you can't sit on that stool without making up the difference yourself.

This is a dramatic shift from one generation to the next, and our culture has not quite accepted these new responsibilities—and risks. The fact is that if you're in your 50s or 60s, you should expect to live through more financial crashes, all with the potential to deliver a blow to your retirement. Just from 1987 to 2017, there were four such crashes. But, today's retirees are unique in that they tend to lack a steady pension when those financial meltdowns occur. **This puts retirees at more risk than ever.** Where should they invest to weather the financial storms and keep their retirement safe?

Responsibilities for Retirement Savings Plans

	Pension	401(k)
Contributions	The **employer** contributed as part of a benefits package that employees earned from a long career of serving the company.	The **employee** contributes to the plan and combining it with their own prudent savings and investments. Employer may match contributions.
Investment strategy	The **employer** hired a reputable pension manager, usually a trained financial advisement firm, to use conservative strategies for reliable returns. If returns are less than expected, the employer accepts all the risks.	The **employee** must develop a working understanding of investment management. They weigh the pros and cons of various mutual funds, select what they feel is best, and determine their own retirement time horizon.
Longevity	An **employer** agrees to pay a qualifying employee's pension for the remainder of the employee's life.	The **employee** faces the uncertainty that the accumulated funds may not last for life.

Your Own Pension Plan

If you are part of the rising group of millions of Americans without pension coverage, one way to rethink your retirement is to use your savings—including your 401(k) if you have one—to fund your own type of pension plan.

Pensions are great when they're offered by your employer, but when it all boils down, what is a pension? It is reliable "mailbox money" that, along with Social Security, can help you meet your costs of living like housing, food, utilities, property taxes, and other expenses that don't stop when your employment does.

CBS News, in talking about stock market ups and downs, reported that the best thing retirees can do is "develop sources of retirement income that don't drop if the stock market crashes" and use those retirement paychecks to "cover most or all of your basic living expenses."[16] So where else, other than pensions, can you find retirement income?

Rethink Recap: Are You Shopping for Car Parts at a Craft Store?

There comes a time in every worker's life when it's more important than ever to protect what they have earned up until that point. As they near retirement, the clock is running out. Not only do they have less opportunities to earn new money, but also they need to leverage what they can out of the money they already have. And yet, even though their lives are dramatically shifting gears, their money tends to not shift gears at all. It stays in the same place: Wall Street.

Can Wall Street alone provide solutions that can guarantee income like a pension? No. Instead, powerful brokers will say, "We will try to grow your money faster than you can spend it!" The truth is that even in a "diversified" portfolio, **Wall Street can grow your money, but it can also lose it just as well**—the risk factor is simply too high for all of your money. Wall Street has a specialty, and that's taking risks for returns. Why are investors looking for safety from a risk-taker? It's like shopping for car parts at a craft store. You're not likely to find what you need, and in fact, you might end up with an impractical (but maybe nice looking) car repair attempt if that's the only place you look. Reliable car parts are just not what a craft store offers.

Don't try to buy safety at a risk shop. Wall Street makes a great product; however, when it comes to allotting a portion of your portfolio to be secure for retirement and generate income for your needs, keep in mind that guaranteed safety is not what Wall Street has for sale. As you approach retirement, rethink risk and meet with a financial professional who is willing to look at the best available retirement solutions. There are safer options out there that can create a pension-like income stream, but it's not from Wall Street. But what are those options? How can you evaluate if a financial product provides the safety you need?

Chapter 2:
The Dynamic Duo

Main Ideas:

- **What is true portfolio safety? Where can you find it and how much should you have?**
- **A simple age-based rule can guide you to the right balance of risk and safety for your savings.**
- **Historically, stocks and bonds were the typical answer for that combination of risk and safety.**
- **How are bonds performing today, and what does that mean for your retirement?**

We've heard it since we were children:
"Don't put all your eggs in one basket."

It's one of the most frequently repeated English idioms. When translated for non-native English speakers, it's usually explained as:

Don't count on any one thing to safeguard everything.
Don't risk it all on success in one area.
Don't put all your savings in only one venture.

Asset allocation, or how you arrange your money, is the classic epitome of this proverb—don't put all your *nest egg* in one basket. This idea, called portfolio diversification, fits the idiom so well that it seems common sense. Surprisingly, it only became a common practice in the 1950s, following the release of the 1952 book *Portfolio Selection*, written by American economist Dr. Harry Markowitz. His idea, "Modern Portfolio Theory," asserts that to minimize volatility and maximize gains, investors should use a mix of financial assets. In the simplest form, the standard practice interpretation means a combination of risk and safety. Markowitz knew you shouldn't put all your eggs in one basket, and calls to diversify your investments were his legacy. Talk about someone who truly made an effort to rethink retirement, and investing in general. Markowitz won the Nobel Prize in Economics for his theory and its contribution to the world of investments.

In your growth or risk "basket," you can have stocks (also called equities), business ventures, and other opportunities where an investor has potential for both growth and losses. Meanwhile, your safety "basket" should include financial assets that offer principal protection, like

Certificate of Deposits (CDs), bonds, and fixed annuities.

These safe money assets offer two main attributes that are highly valuable to any portfolio, but become more necessary in retirement. I call these my "P-Rs of Safe Money." You may have heard of "P.R." in the fitness world, which means "personal record." It's a benchmark for individual achievement and being your best. Similarly, these two P-Rs are an evaluation standard for achieving a critical level of protection in retirement planning.

P-Rs of Safe Money

Protection & Reliability: Your investment should be protected from ever sustaining any losses from the stock market. This protection should provide you peace of mind and reliability.

Payment & Return: You should have an ability to receive regular income as well as receive reasonable returns over time, at least ahead of inflation.

So how much should you allocate to each basket? You invest in risk money what you can afford to lose. But how do you know what you can afford to lose, and how does that amount change as you move toward retirement? A good general rule is to use the "Rule of 100."

Good Thinking: Rule of 100

_____ % of my assets that should be in safe money

(my age)

100 - _____ % = _____ % of my portfolio that can be

(my age)   in risk money

The Rule of 100

Like many retirement advisors, I am a proponent of the Rule of 100. In this guideline, you simply think of your age as a percentage of money that should be allocated in safe money. Depending on your personal tolerance for risk, your investment objectives, and time horizon, the remaining percentage can be invested in risk money ventures.

For example, a 60 year-old should have at least 60% of their savings allocated to safe money. No more than 40% should be invested in risk money on Wall Street.

Brilliant investment legend John Bogle, who founded the multi-billion dollar Vanguard Group, believed investors should own "roughly your age in bonds" or safe assets. He reasoned that the wisdom in this is "almost self-evident":

> *"As we age, we usually have 1.) more wealth to protect, 2.) less time to recoup severe losses, 3.) greater need for income, and 4.) perhaps an increased nervousness as markets jump around. These factors suggest more bonds as we age."*[17]

This rule is simple, but highly useful. Why? Though it's not an exact science, it highlights the need for increasing protection as individuals move through life.

Switching Gears

If safe money is so important, why not put more into safe money earlier on? In your 30s and 40s, your savings needs to accumulate. You're growing and advancing in a career and alongside that, your money from that career needs to be growing and advancing, too. Historically, Wall Street has great long-term growth for those who can withstand the turbulence. During your early earning years, you have enough time to weather financial storms and to keep reinvesting.

However, as you near retirement, it is critical to switch gears from growth mode to safety mode. That's not to say that your portfolio should leave the market entirely. Stock market investments remain an important part of many retirement portfolios, so long as they are allocated to put the emphasis on safe, reliable retirement income *first*. As I like to say, **'Safety is best, then invest the rest.'** That falls right in line with the Rule of 100.

I recently had the opportunity to meet with Ed, one of my clients, soon after he turned ninety years old. The meeting was unique, not because of the client's age, but because he brought every one of his six children to the meeting. Each of them were in town for Ed's birthday celebration. It was standing room only, except for Ed, of course, who was sharp as a tack as we talked about his financial standing and his savings portfolio. His caring children wanted to make sure that their father was receiving the best advice and that his financial affairs were in order. We reviewed Ed's asset allocation, which was aligned based on the Rule of 100. His children were very pleased to see that the vast majority of their father's account was not only safe from losses, but also receiving competitive returns.

His modest savings had grown to provide Ed with monthly income that, combined with Social Security, would continue to give him income security every month for the rest of his life. He also had funds that were growing steadily and would never decline in value as part of a guaranteed legacy to his children. And a very small portion of money that Ed could afford to lose was invested in the stock market to offer growth potential for himself or his heirs.

Of course, depending on your unique financial situation, including your assets, your liabilities, and your financial goals during retirement, your particular allocation could be different than this general guideline, which is why it is always wise to meet with a trained expert who specializes in retirement planning.

Meeting with a retirement advisor, adjusting your portfolio based on the Rule of 100 as you age, and adapting that guideline to your needs and preferences are ways to have more peace of mind and fewer surprises in retirement.

We Go Together Like...

Peanut butter and jelly.
Bacon and eggs.
Salt and pepper
Milk and cookies.
Stocks and bonds.

These classic pairs have distinctly different, maybe even opposite, components. But it's undeniable that they are stronger together than on their own. Why are stocks and bonds a dynamic duo? Stocks represent the risk money, satisfying a portfolio's need to have an element of higher growth potential. Bonds, on the other hand, are traditionally presented as safe money. Why?

Good Thinking: Bonds 101

A bond is like a loan contract where you are the lender. They are issued by corporations or governments, such as the U.S. Treasury ("treasuries") or state, city, county or other local governments (municipal bonds or "munis"). These entities use your money, giving you interest payments in the meantime, usually once or twice per year. Typical bonds have a maturity date, or set expiration date when the debt is due back to you in full and the interest payments end.

Bonds have those desirable P-Rs of Safe Money, which offer a counterpoint to stock's greater risk:

1) **Protection & Reliability:** As long as you are investing with an entity that is unlikely to default, like a U.S. Treasury Bond, and you hold the bond until maturity, you will receive your *entire* investment back at the end of your bond period (or when your bond reaches "maturity").

2) **Payment & Returns:** You'll see returns on your investment throughout the bond period. These periodic payments are called "interest payments" (or "coupon payments"). They are established up-front when you invest in the bond. For example, your $10,000 bond may issue you $250 annually. This means your interest rate is 2.50%.

Now, bonds have their downsides, as they can be more complicated to buy and manage, and have limited options for liquidity, or pulling out your money, if you are in a pinch and need your investment back. But historically, bonds have been a worthwhile part of a diversified portfolio because they offer the P-Rs of Safe Money not found in stocks. So, when your investment advisor says that a portion of your portfolio is in "bond funds," this is sure to be safe, right? Not so fast, unfortunately. This is one of the most important misunderstandings in the investment world today.

Bond Funds: Risk Money in Disguise

A bond, as we've learned, is a debt security that pays a regular interest payment. Investors can also enjoy principal protection and recoup their investment in full when the bond reaches maturity.

However, a "bond fund" (or sometimes, "fixed-income fund") offered by Wall Street does not always have those P-Rs of Safe Money that you can expect from bonds. Bond funds are a complex financial product, but an important one to understand. Bond funds are simply a basket of bonds that are *turned into a mutual or exchange-traded fund*, which pays its holders interest payments. These funds are popular because they are much easier to buy and sell than directly held bonds, and provide an excellent opportunity to diversify your portfolio. But, as a general rule, do all bond funds satisfy the P-Rs of Safe Money?

1. No **P**rotection & **R**eliability
2. Uncertain **P**ayment & **R**eturn

No Protection & Reliability

Despite their user-friendly features, they are missing arguably the most important element of the P-Rs of Safe Money: they offer no principal protection. With a bond fund, you don't own a bond, "you own mutual fund shares," reports CNBC.[18] "**There is never a day that you are**

assured of getting back 100% of your principal." This is because like any mutual or exchange-traded fund, they are traded like baseball cards between buyers and sellers, allowing the fund value to fluctuate daily.

Another glaring issue: unreliability due to interest rate sensitivity. When interest rates rise, any newly-issued bonds will have better interest payments than older bonds issued during lower interest rates. So, to help sell those mutual funds packaged with those older bonds, the mutual funds go on "sale" and have a lower value. Some analysts report that in certain bond funds, even a 1% increase in interest rates can result *in a 10% loss or more in the bond fund value.*

I recently met with a new client named Jack, and as part of our first conversation, I asked him if he had any particular questions or concerns I could help with. He said, "I just know I need to move my money to something safer. Right now, I'm in a lot of bond funds. Did you know they're not actually real bonds? I know they're not as safe as bonds because my account value keeps dropping every time interest rates go up!" I replied, "Yes, I do know that, and I'm glad you know that too!" As Jack realized, any financial product that can decline in value is not safe money.

Bonds and Interest Rates

Bonds have two aspects: the value and the interest payment (just like a savings account has both an account value and an interest payment). U.S. Federal Reserve interest rates affect both aspects.

1.) Bond *interest payments* mirror the *interest rate* environment. Since the market collapse in 2001, our Federal Reserve has created an unprecedented, about two-decade-long, low interest rate environment to spur on economic growth. We're motivated to move our money out of savings accounts and instead buy homes, cars, and anything we can buy on a low-interest balance transfer credit card! Addicted to these low interest rates, we may not mind that our bonds and other safe money instruments do not have the interest payment that they used to. Just look at the 1979 bond below: can you imagine a 10.125% interest payment? Over the last decade, typical bonds have returned less than 3% a year, with some short-term U.S. Treasuries hovering just above 0%!

2.) When interest rates go up, suddenly brand new bonds are more attractive, because they pay the higher interest payment. So if someone wanted to sell their older, low-interest-payment bond, they would need to put it on "sale" and cut the price of their bond, lowering its value.

A 1979 15-year U.S. Treasury Bond with 10 1/8% yield. Source: National Archives.

Uncertain Payment & Return

Historically, bond funds have provided consistent returns above 4% a year. This explains why billions of dollars are invested in bond funds and managed by Wall Street firms. But, because of our low interest rate environment, the actual interest payments from the individual bonds within the bond funds are very low, which causes a low return in these bond mutual funds. Bonds have a constant, reliable return that is set when you purchase the bond. But bond funds? In this wild interest rate environment, there is no way to know how long the Federal Government will keep rates low and what returns you will earn. Safe money should at least have an option for a guaranteed return.

Investment analyst Scott Colyer explains, "There is a huge difference between bond funds and individual bonds. Some suggest that they're not even the same asset class, because bond funds react so differently to market forces. Now more than ever, with interest rate [fluctuations], investors need to understand the difference."[18]

Rethinking your Bond Funds

Bond funds can be useful financial tools, because 1) they are a fund with interest or dividend payments and 2) these mutual funds are a collection of *bonds* instead of *stocks*, which can mean less risk in your portfolio. **But "less risk" is not "no risk"**! I gladly recommend bond funds to many clients, as long as they are generally allocated where they belong: in the risk money portion of their portfolio, where they have limited exposure in the event of a loss.

The trouble with bond funds happens when retirees assume that all bond funds are safe money, perhaps due to the inclusion of the word "bond," a safe money asset, in their name. A recent Fortune article warned, **"In the fixed income [or "safe money"] side of portfolios, [retirees] are taking equity-like risk with bond funds, guaranteeing that the protection from volatility that bonds offer does not show up when it is most needed."**[19] Simply put, if you substitute bond funds for safe money, your portfolio will be lacking in the especially critical **P**rotection & **R**eliability, **P**ayment & **R**eturns in retirement.

Rethink Recap: Safe Money That's Actually Safe

We have an issue on our hands in modern retirement planning. We see the wisdom of having both risk and safe money, and we can use the elegant simplicity of the Rule of 100 to get there. But where do we go for safe money? How do we satisfy the Rule of 100 for our portfolios, especially after age 50, that tipping point when we shift gears from the majority of our money in risk to the majority in safety?

Unfortunately:

- *Bonds*, which do satisfy the safe money standards, can have poor liquidity and have had nearly two decades of lower-than-usual interest payments due to our low interest rate environment.

- *Bond funds*, which also currently suffer from low returns, do not fully meet the requirements for P-Rs of Safe Money. In particular, they lack the principal protection that safe money ought to provide.

In an Op-ed for *Money* magazine, Ruth Davis Konisburg, Director at Arden Asset Management complained, "I would love to find a bond fund that could be both a safe haven and provide steady returns, but I just don't think that exists."[20]

Interestingly, "safe haven" of protection with "steady returns" sounds like the P-Rs of Safe Money! Contrary to this advisor's belief, do these combinations in fact exist? Experts agree that it does not exist on Wall Street, and to be honest, it's unfair to expect Wall Street to do everything. As I discussed in Chapter 1, Wall Street has its advantages, but it has never been in the "safety" business. So, who is in the safety business?

Chapter 3:
Axe the Annuity Anxiety

Main Ideas:

- **Set aside what you may have heard about annuities of the past. Simply put, today's annuities are for today's retirees.**
- **Have you ever heard of the poem, "The Blind Men and the Elephant"? Like the elephant, annuities have myriad qualities and it can be easy to misunderstand their features and benefits.**

Know safety, no risk.
No safety, know risk.

If Wall Street isn't in the safety business, then who is? The answer is actually closer than you might think. Where do we go to find peace of mind for our valuables—our homes, cars, even our family heirlooms? Insurance companies. Since the first insurance companies formed in 1666 to protect homes from fire (even to the point of insurance companies maintaining their own fire fighter brigades), insurance has offered assurance that we can protect what matters to us. Part of what makes the U.S. great is that we have trust in our ability to insure things, and can find insurance for nearly anything. Companies can even insure a promotional $100,000 basketball half-court shot, in that slim 2% chance that a lucky person makes it!

Yes, at times, insurance can be frustrating, especially when we battle with phone agents over healthcare. But, as long as you have taken steps to protect your belongings, you can be given powerful assurances no matter what lies in your future. Were you in an accident and totaled the car? If fully insured, you are given funds for a replacement. Did your house burn down due to an electrical fire? With insurance, you can recoup the value of your home and goods. Have you suffered the untimely death of a loved one? While nothing can take their place, those with life insurance are given some reparation for this serious loss to help them move forward. Insurance literally means "to make sure." It gives us the confidence to live our lives with more security and less fear.

In the world of finance and retirement planning, insurance companies can protect yet another valuable in your life: your savings, and more specifically, your retirement. These products are called *annuities*, and due to unfortunate misconceptions, misunderstandings, and even some misuse, these powerful tools are often overlooked and require rethinking for comprehensive retirement planning.

Annuities 101

Let's clear up a few of the misconceptions about what annuities are, and what they are not.

In the past, most annuities were often used as a single lump-sum payment to an insurance company in exchange for a safe, but low return. These annuities provided set payments, usually for life, but acquired a reputation for low returns and restrictions. Fortunately, in the last twenty years, insurance companies have gone back to the drawing board to offer better (less complicated and more flexible) annuities that can provide income and growth throughout your retirement years.

Today, annuities are more commonly used as a place to keep money safe and still provide growth opportunities. That place to keep money safe is with a reputable insurance company who only wants to hold your money for a certain period of time, and in exchange, will give you desirable benefits. One such annuity like this is called a *deferred fixed* annuity, which offers the benefit of a *fixed* or guaranteed interest rate for a specific time. Payments or a complete payout from the annuity to you are *deferred* until a later date.

What are the basic terms of a *deferred fixed* annuity contract? In an annuity contract, you agree to:

- Provide a deposit or sum of money that will be held by the insurance company.
- Start withdrawals in the future after the account value has grown.
- Often agree to not withdraw your entire lump sum of money for a certain time period. These terms vary, but are generally between five and ten years, after which you'll have full access to all your funds. Typically after the first year, 10% of the account balance is available for you to withdraw each year.
- Consent that if you withdraw more than contractually allowed (usually 10% of the annuity value) in a given year, you would be subject to a penalty or surrender charge for breaking the contract. These charges can vary and tend to decline the longer your money is on deposit.

Insurance companies agree to:

- Hold your deposit in cash and highly rated cash-in-kind (easily converted to cash) investments, like U.S. Treasuries and investment-grade bonds.
- Use the interest from those bonds for your guaranteed returns, principal protection, and other income generating features.

- Grant full access to your funds after you have met the contract's time requirement.
- Facilitate special tax treatment on your deposit. For example, many annuities are not taxed until you withdraw the funds.
- Provide a death benefit, usually the current contract or account value, payable to your heirs with no charges or fees.

It is important to remember that this is only a basic deferred fixed annuity template. There are well over one hundred types of fixed annuity contracts offered by reputable insurance companies, each with their own term lengths, growth options, and other income-generating features. It is key to work with a qualified retirement planner who can recommend the right strategy for you.

But What Are Fixed Annuities Not?

Fixed annuities are *not* a bank savings or liquid stock market investment account where you go for any of your quick cash needs. They are not a "get rich quick" investment opportunity. Fixed annuities are best for patient investors, with medium to long-term holding expectations, who want to see a safe, but steady, uninterrupted stream of returns or income over time.

Because annuities are offered by insurance companies, they are different from other investment vehicles. My mentor, Jed, would tell me to take off my "investment hat" and put on my "deposit hat." This is because fixed annuities do not have investments' susceptibility for both downside risk and rapid fluctuation. Rather, like a deposit, fixed annuities can provide powerful protections from your money ever losing value, as well as stable growth.

Banks vs. Insurance Companies

One question I'm often asked is if insurance company annuities are that different from a bank certificate of deposit (CD). This is a great question. Let me answer by comparing banks and insurance companies.

Deposits at a bank are very common and well understood. You want safety and access to your money, and the bank wants returns through interest rates on the loans they issue, such as small business, home, or auto loans.

Banks also invest your money in the stock market, or in their own real estate ventures. And yes, they

Good Thinking: The Legal Reserve Requirement

The legal reserve, or statutory capital reserve ratio, is the minimum amount of cash or cash equivalents that an institution must hold of their customers' deposits. This can include cash in a vault, U.S. Treasury notes or bonds, and other cash equivalents.

Legal Reserve Requirement (cash or cash-in-kind) on $100,000:
    Commercial bank: 3-11% = $3,000-$11,000
    Insurance company: 101%-108% = $101,000-$108,000

can even run into trouble by overextending their investment portfolio, as they did in 2008. They manage to overextend since **banks are only legally required to hold onto 3 to 11% of your deposit**.

We trust banks in large part because of the Federal Deposit Insurance Corporation (FDIC). If your bank fails and is unable to meet their obligation to you and their other depositors, the federal government will step in and make you whole up to $250,000. Although that amount was only recently increased from $100,000 due to the 2008 crisis, we still generally have a good opinion of banks.

What about insurance companies? When you purchase an annuity contract from a reputable insurance company, the money is **not loaned or put in risk money investments**. Insurance companies have a legal reserve requirement to **keep at least 101 to 108% of your annuity contract money on hand in cash or cash-in-kind investments**, such as U.S. Treasury and investment-grade bonds. Knowing how much they'll earn on those bonds is how insurance actuaries determine how much you'll earn on your interest payments. This is how annuities typically pay a little better interest than CDs: Annuities earn their interest through reliable bonds, rather than interest rates on bank loans.

Do insurance companies have FDIC insurance? No, because insurance companies already operate under insurance reserve requirements. They don't need insurance: they *are* the insurance! Over 100% of your deposit is already on hand in case of trouble, compared to only 3 to 11% of your deposit at a bank.

CDs are similar to annuities in that both offer you a fixed return when you essentially loan your money to the bank or insurance company. For deposits of more than $250,000, annuities are typically best due to an insurance company's far greater legal reserve requirement. Annuities, unlike CDs, also offer other tax planning benefits, death benefits, lifetime income benefits, and other options.

Better than a Bond?

These all sound like great features, but do fixed annuities satisfy the criteria of P-Rs of Safe Money?

Fortunately, a fixed annuity has many similarities to directly held bonds. Yet in some ways, they are better than bonds: fixed annuities have the "P-Rs of Safe Money," plus more liquidity. After the first year, annuity contracts usually allow the holder to access 10% of the total deposit each year without giving up your benefits. On the other hand, "the only way to access money from a bond, other than a fixed coupon payment, is to sell," reports U.S. News and World Report.[21]

P-Rs of Safe Money: Bonds vs. Fixed Annuities

	Bond	Fixed Annuity
Protection & Reliability	Yes, bonds are guaranteed by the bond issuer (such as the U.S. government). Funds will be returned to you, plus interest, guaranteed, if bond is held until maturity.	Yes, annuities are guaranteed by the insurance company and their legal reserve requirement. Funds are returned to you, plus interest, if held until end of contract.
Payment & Return	Yes, interest rate is set before you invest. Payment is based on a fixed coupon schedule.	Yes, rate of return and any other benefits are set before you sign the contract. Typical contracts allow you to withdraw funds penalty-free each year (usually 10% of the account value per year).

You might say that fixed annuities are the best of both bonds and bond funds. That's not to say that it's not worth considering talking to your financial advisor about adding bonds or bond funds to your portfolio, as they have excellent features that are right for many investors. But for those who are looking for a simultaneous combination of safe money and respectable liquidity, fixed annuities are a worthwhile addition to a retirement savings plan.

Why the Annuity Angst?

Growing up, my parents had a saying attached to the family refrigerator, probably the most highly-viewed space in our home. It read:

"What is popular is not always right,
What is right is not always popular."

Fixed annuities are a useful financial tool. They are, or would be, the right tool for millions of retirees because they provide safety, steady returns, and are issued through the same principles that insure other valuables in our lives. In fact, due to legal reserve, insurance companies are arguably safer than banks. Despite all of this, annuities are not popular in some circles, especially of Wall Street investment advisors. Why?

I blame the negativity on three reasons:
1.) **Wall Street bias and fixation on returns.** The discussion in Chapter 1 stresses that more money is flowing into Wall Street than ever before. Wall Street wants to keep all they have under management to collect fees, even if, based on age or other factors, you ought to have more safety and deescalate risk. So over the years, they've made

phenomenal attempts to control the narrative. We see the sensational headlines, like "Avoid All Annuities" or "Why Annuities are Bad for Everyone" from, unsurprisingly, 24-hour Wall Street news channels or websites. We also tend to fixate on returns, and when Wall Street is doing well, we ignore safer options—that is, until Wall Street volatility comes back.

2.) **Annuity Incompatibility.** Some negativity about annuities is perhaps due to a mismatch between the annuity and the contract holder. I'm a true believer that it's good to have options out there—sure, an annuity might not be right for your situation, but its features could be ideal for someone else. This is why it's important to not get your annuity from just any insurance salesperson, but someone who is licensed and has retirement planning expertise, who can weigh all the available options and suggest the right strategy for your retirement income and legacy planning needs.

3.) **Variable and Immediate Annuities.** Above all, most of the negativity on annuities is due to two products that require some caution: Variable Annuities and Immediate Annuities.

Have you heard any of the following?

- *"Annuities aren't safe! I know someone who lost money on their annuity."*
  While <u>fixed</u> annuities have <u>fixed</u> values and 100% principle protection, <u>variable</u> annuities have <u>variable</u> values, and there is a risk you can lose money. Variable annuities are typically tied to a stock market component, such as a mutual fund, in a sub-account. These sub-accounts can rise and fall just like any mutual fund. In retirement, you need a portion of your portfolio that is disconnected from risk for you to count on for your living expenses. Variable annuities are **<u>not</u>** safe money and in the Rule of 100, should be categorized with your other risk money ventures, like stocks.

- *"I want something without annual fees. All annuities have fees, right?"*
  While most fixed annuities do not have annual fees, variable annuities tend to have these fees and more. There are mortality and expense (M&E) fees, investment advisory fees, rider fees, and sub-account fees. I've seen some variable annuities with fees in the 5 to 6% range per year. In my opinion, these fees are excessive and unacceptable.

- *"But what about when I die? Will my family lose all the money I paid?"*

This only would happen in what are often called *single life immediate annuities,* carefully selected because the contract owner has a critical need for income immediately and continuing throughout *their lifetime only.* They may be in a situation like Gladys in the beginning of this book and facing dire consequences like bankruptcy and choose to liquidate an asset, like their home, to provide a safe income with increasing payouts to protect against inflation. This type of annuity dominated the industry over 20 years ago, which led to the stories of principal loss (insurance company keeping your money) and unexpected death. In many pensions, they still are extensively used as the highest monthly income option for a retiree, but need to be carefully considered by the owner and a retirement advisor.

Outside of these single life annuities, almost all deferred fixed annuities include a complete return of your principal and earnings (minus your withdrawals) upon your death.

Last year I met with Marie, a woman nearing retirement who was referred to me by a friend. She said that she went to her long-time financial advisor and said, "I'm up at night, nervous about this market. Please help me." He suggested a variable annuity, which he could managed that offered some guarantees of income, but did not offer any principal protection—not at all what she asked for. She wanted a safer option, but 1) he didn't have any safe products to offer her from his Wall Street firm, and 2) he didn't want to lose her business. He was likely doing *his* best given the circumstances and constraints of his firm, but not what was best for *her*.

Marie's friend suggested she listen to me on the radio. After that, she visited me and we put together a safe money plan. Marie expressed how grateful she was that she did her research to find what she was really looking for, because now she can literally and figuratively rest easy.

When it comes to negativity about annuities, consider the source. And, if a retirement advisor suggests an annuity, do your due diligence and ensure you are signing on the line for the right type of annuity for your needs. It's confusing that variable annuities, which are so different from deferred fixed annuities, are even considered annuities. It's almost as head scratching as tomatoes being classified as a fruit: If I judged *all* fruits based on the characteristics of tomatoes, I would have a very skewed interpretation of what fruits really are! And yet, nearly every day, I meet with people who have a perspective on annuities that lacks the complete picture.

"The Blind Men and the Elephant." Charles Maurice Stebbins & Mary H. Coolidge (1909). *Golden Treasury Readers: Primer*, American Book Co. (New York).

Annuities and the Elephant

Nineteenth century American poet John Godfrey Saxe wrote the famous 1872 poem, "The Blind Men and the Elephant." In the poem, six men approached an elephant and, using their own observations, declared boldly to their peers what it was. However, due to being visually impaired, their conclusions were incorrect. One, feeling the wiggling trunk, said an elephant is nothing more than a snake; another, touching the tusk, concluded that an elephant is another name for a spear; one more, touching only the elephant's rough, broad side, assumed that an elephant is simply a wall.

The poem reads,

And so these [blind] men, disputed loud and long,
Each in his own opinion, exceeding stiff and strong,
Though each was partly in the right,
And all were in the wrong!

I think what's important to recognize from the poem is that these individuals weren't ignorant. They were speaking from their own experience, but didn't realize they lacked the whole picture. Imagine what they could have gained by talking to a zoologist! An expert could have pointed out the aspects they missed or misinterpreted.

If you're considering an annuity, a retirement advisor with the right training and experience in annuities can be that expert, offering a more complete picture of what annuities are and aren't.

In addition to the right annuity product, individuals approaching retirement also need:

- **Sound planning timing.** Deferred fixed annuities involve certain benefits for specific contract lengths. The sooner you come in to meet with an advisor, the more opportunities that may be available to you. For example, annuities that pay higher interest and offer better guaranteed income options, but have long-term lengths, would likely be unadvisable for older retirees.

- **Highly rated insurance companies.** As a matter of common sense, industry recommendations encourage contracts with companies that are B++ *at a minimum,* but usually sticking to A range is best. Your advisor can give you all this information to help you find the best products from the best insurance providers.

When it all comes down to it, getting the right annuity is like shopping for the right car. Yes, it can be complicated and require some research, but the benefits and freedom from owning the *right* car make it all worthwhile. And, to help guard against a lemon, a trusted mechanic looks under the hood for a thorough inspection. They suggest the best vehicle, with reliable features to enhance your life, just as a trusted retirement advisor can do for you.

Rethink Recap: Reconsider Annuities

Why is safety important to you? What lengths are you willing to go to keep your retirement safe?

One favorite client story is from Steve, a retired paramedic. In his 50s, doctors diagnosed him with a congenital heart condition, and he had a successful surgery. Healing took longer than his 12-week job-protected leave, so to earn his spot back on the squad—along with the retirement and pension he had built up over his 28-year career—he had to redo his physical qualification tests with much younger recruits, all coming off a grueling recovery. His final test required completing a boot camp-like obstacle course in seven minutes, and he passed with just one second to spare! After literally fighting to restore his career, with full retirement benefits and pension, he told me, "I almost lost these benefits once, I'm not putting them at risk again." Like the proverb at the beginning of this chapter, this is coming from someone who "knows safety" and "knows risk" from his career as a first responder. After all he experienced, he wanted a retirement advisor and retirement solutions that provided guarantees. Today, he enjoys monthly payments from his annuity, and knows he's protected the retirement he fought for.

One way to rethink your retirement is to rethink how you are assuring your own hard-won retirement. In a world of uncertainties, the right annuities are designed to offer powerful peace of mind that for at least this aspect of your life, you no longer will "know risk."

Chapter 4:
Don't Risk for Rewards

Main Ideas:

- Engrained in our culture, and in the stock market, is the idea that you must assume risks to earn rewards. Is that always true?
- A relatively new annuity, the fixed indexed annuity, has changed the conversation around growth and risk.
- If you are interested in competitive returns tied to U.S. stock market growth, but are too close to retirement to take hefty risks, fixed indexed annuities may be the right product for you.

Think back: How old were you when you were first told, "No pain, no gain"? Or maybe, "No risk, no reward?"

It came for me when I was in the third grade and my family dared me to try a new theme park roller coaster. I was terrified. I looked straight up at the

Roller coaster like the one from my childhood. Photography by Stefan Scheer (2007)[22]

twisted steel, with piercing screams each time passengers whooshed by, and every part of my barely-tall-enough frame wanted to run.

"No guts, no glory!" they said, "What are you, chicken?" I was *not* about to be called a chicken, so I strapped into the harness and took a chance.

It seems that from childhood, we are raised with this idea that the only way to get what we want out of life is to take risks. Proverbs say,

"Fortune favors the bold."

"Who dares, wins."

"Ships are safe in harbor, but that's not what ships are made for."

These ideas dominate our culture. When you think about it, you might even say we glamorize risk.

We see it in the heart-pounding action that keeps us glued to the movie screen. And, of course, on stock market news channels where analysts weigh in on big business deals and excitedly talk about hot stock buys. Even after closing bell, the urgency in their voices keeps us on the edge of our seats.

In all this, we get a clear message: risk is thrilling. Perhaps that is why it's hard to reduce our positions in the stock market when it comes time to do so. Recently a client told me about their friends who, as they neared retirement in their late 50s, left their entire savings allocated in the stock market where it had been for years. "It's exciting to see how well it has performed lately," this couple rationalized. "If it keeps going, we can retire early." Unfortunately, that conversation occurred in late 2007. Like Gladys from early on in the book, by late 2008, they had lost over 40% of their account value. Instead of early retirement, both continued working to recoup losses.

As we near retirement, we can't tolerate risk as we once did. The Rule of 100 is straightforward in that our age is the percentage of our money that should be in low- or no-risk investments. The greater our age, the greater the percentage in safety so that we can live on what we have, especially when we are no longer earning employment income. We need to shift priorities. Remember: safety is best, *then* invest the rest.

Rethinking How to Win

What about this instead:

- *Rethink that Wall Street is the only vehicle for asset growth.*
- *Rethink the stock market myth that you must risk to have gains.*
- *Rethink that belief that you ought to ride Wall Street's roller coaster and endure the downs in order to enjoy any ups.*

Speaking of which, are you curious to know what happened when I rode that roller coaster as a kid? My head bounced around in that safety harness like it was in a pinball machine! I was terrified on the ride, but even more miserable afterward when I could hardly move due to a pulled muscle. I spent the rest of the day on a park bench in a neck brace while my siblings rode rides.

I'll always remember the ride home. Each shared their favorite ride of the day, and most everyone said it was the kiddie go-cart racers. What? It wasn't a ride with thrills and spills, it wasn't anything you would find on the theme park advertisements, it was just a simple ride that everyone laughed and enjoyed (except for me on that park bench).

What if we simply had fun without danger, growth without risk, safety with returns? It feels like a contradiction, especially after all we have been told in childhood. So how do you get growth without risk?

Enter **fixed indexed annuities**, one of the most innovative financial products of the last two decades. These are relative newcomers, but in high demand. In 1997, less than two years after they debuted, there were $3 billion in new fixed indexed annuity contracts that year. By 2008, there were $26 billion in new contracts, and by 2017, that figure doubled to $58 billion, in accounts where individuals enjoy both safety and returns. How?

How Do They Work?

To start, fixed *indexed* annuities are still, at their core, fixed annuities:

- Issued by an insurance company that legally holds your principal account value
- Safeguarded from risk exposure
- Offers account growth potential and periodic payments.

So, what makes them unique? In a fixed indexed annuity, your interest payment is not limited to a fixed yield per year like in a fixed annuity; rather, you have the potential for higher returns, linked to *stock market index performance*.

One common stock market-linked strategy provides an interest payment of **50% of the S&P**

Good to Know: Fixed Indexed Annuity

A Fixed Indexed Annuity (FIA) is a hybrid annuity product that offers the owner or annuitant protection in down markets, but opportunities for growth in up markets. It blends the safety and reliability that can come from a fixed annuity with interest linked to a stock market index.

500's performance in a given year. In that scenario, say the S&P 500 was up 8% for the year. In your indexed annuity, you get a 4% return—an anxiety-free gain, because remember, *your principle amount is never at risk in the stock market.* Jed would refer to this as "gain and retain." Once you earn an interest amount in your indexed annuity, you keep it.

In that same scenario, if the S&P 500 declines 25% the following year, you don't give back any gains or suffer any losses. Your account remains at 100% of the value for the year prior and you would earn 0.00% in interest for that year.

Explain It Like I'm Five Years Old

Remember the popular "___ For Dummies" books of the 1990s? Today, the equivalent are online forums called "Explain Like I'm Five." Doctors, chemists, and all kinds of professionals take complexities in their fields and make the information accessible so anyone can learn.

Here's my attempt: Fixed indexed annuities are a one-way financial staircase designed for people in or nearing retirement. Each year (and your money is not withdrawn from the account), it will only go up with the stock market or stay steady if the market falls without ever going back down.

To see if a fixed indexed annuity is right for part of your retirement savings, there is no substitute for meeting with a retirement advisor and discussing your financial goals. For millions of Americans, especially those interested in a piece of American economic growth, fixed indexed annuities are an option worth exploring—an opportunity for gain without pain.

"I Want the Impossible"

Who are fixed indexed annuities right for? Not long ago, a new client met with me and said she wanted to level with me. She was retired and nervous about the future of the stock market for

A fixed annuity is like a continual one-way staircase: you can go up or perhaps stay the same, but you cannot go down in value, even if the stock market does.

her money. She was looking for something that could check all her boxes, which were:

☑ Low- or no-risk
☑ Growth opportunities
☑ Potential to keep up with inflation
☑ Ability to make withdrawals over time

She chuckled and said, "Hey, I want the impossible!" I told her that if she has realistic expectations for both the growth and liquidity, that her dream financial investment was possible after all—through a fixed indexed annuity.

She seemed surprised she had never heard of a fixed indexed annuity before, but as we know, it's Wall Street, not insurance companies, that control the narrative about reliable financial products for retirement. And that narrative is often that annuities have no growth. Because they have no stock market risk, they must have no growth opportunities, right? In short, annuities are just plain boring, right? Wrong!

Even for me, I misunderstood fixed indexed annuities when I was part of a Wall Street-only firm. Why? Because my firm emphasized how important it was to keep clients' assets in Wall Street funds where we could take quarterly management fees. Moving the money from Wall Street to an insurance company would dry up those fees. Many financial advisors live out Upton

Sinclair's wise words, *"It is difficult to get a man to understand something when his salary depends upon his not understanding it."*[23]

Wall Street advisors may disregard fixed indexed annuities because they take away from money under management. In fact, in the mid-2000s, as fixed indexed annuities were making waves, I traveled to a national financial advisement conference. In a break-out educational session called, "Financial Products for Retirement," the instructor kicked off the topic by discussing what he called one of the most exciting financial tools of our time: fixed indexed annuities. Believe it or not, several financial advisors in the audience heard that, grumbled, stood up…. and walked out. They resisted listening to an expert's ideas, even if it may be the right solution for a client someday, because it would move money out from under their management fees. This shows the animosity towards fixed indexed annuities, and annuities in general, that some advisors considered an hour's education on the subject as a waste of their time.

Never Take a Loss

Although it's exciting, fixed indexed annuity's power doesn't only come in its Wall Street participation. Yes, it is appealing to be part of American economic growth, but returns are often only a portion of the index's increase and may even have caps, depending on the annuity product.

One of the greatest benefits is the insulation from losses. One of genius investment guru Warren Buffet's pieces of advice is:
"Rule #1: Never lose money.
Rule #2: Never forget Rule #1."

In a way, this is simplistic at best, insulting at worst. Everyone has lost money, especially those who venture out and take risks. I bet if you paused a minute or two, you could recount your more frustrating money-losing endeavors, probably with vivid detail. Why is it that we remember losses so well? Ever heard of the phrase "losses loom larger than gains"? Behavioral psychologists found that the psychological pain of losing has *twice* the impact as the thrill of winning.[24] These negative experiences have great power on our emotions and our memories.

Who needs Buffet's advice the most? As you near retirement, or if you're already there, there's *no better time* to be protected from losses. Retirees have more immediate income needs than most other investors and have less time to recover. Remember, a 50% loss requires a 100% gain to recover your investment. That typically takes time that most retirees don't have.

Consider the five-year simulation below. With a $100,000 initial investment in the stock market, you may have four years of double-digit gains of 10%, *but a single 30% loss* means that your account will barely recover above your initial investment by the end of Year 5. $102,487 represents an overall 2.49% gain from the $100,000 start.

On the other hand, a $100,000 fixed indexed annuity with a typical 50% market participation rate—earning 50% of the market index each year, but with complete account value protection—ends the simulation with $121,551, a 21.55% 5-year gain.

This is the power of never taking a loss. Through a stock market storm, the simulation with tempered gains, *but total protection from any losses*, has far greater returns—over 8 times the returns in this simulation.

Table 1: Stock Market vs. Fixed Indexed Annuities

	Stock Market Initial Investment $100k		Fixed Indexed Annuity* Initial Investment $100k	
End of Year	Value	Gain/ Loss	Value	Gain/ Loss
1	$110,000	10%	$105,000	5%
2	$121,000	10%	$110,250	5%
3	$84,700	-30%	$110,250	0%
4	$93,170	10%	$115,763	5%
5	$102,487	10%	$121,551	5%
Total	$102,487	2.49%	$121,551	21.55%

*Fixed index annuity with 50% stock market annual participation rate

After a long, productive career of bringing home your "winnings" in income, you need to keep as much as possible of what you have. You need to have opportunities to move forward without the risk of falling backward. **One way to rethink retirement is to recognize that with a fixed indexed annuity, you can participate in Wall Street's gains, but protect your account from ever declining in value.** In a market downturn, when your friends in the market are losing money, you'll have the peace of mind that this portion of your savings will never take a loss.

Experts Weigh In

World-renowned Yale finance professor, Dr. Roger Ibbotson, recently compared fixed indexed annuities, bonds, and stocks and his results rocked the Wall Street world. After all, Dr. Ibbotson is an expert that literally wrote the book on the stock market (it's called *Stocks, Bonds, Bills, and Inflation*, and is an annually updated reference book used by Wall Street firms). When he found that fixed indexed annuities were a powerful, no-risk performance vehicle with advantages over stocks and bonds, financial professionals took notice.

To make his case, he used historical stock market data to generate 90 years (1927-2016) of hypothetical returns for stocks, bonds, and fixed indexed annuities.[25] Large cap stocks (large corporations worth $10 billion or more) had the highest average annualized returns, with about

10% gain. But they also were highly volatile: investors were vulnerable for as much as a 27% loss over three years in his test period. Meanwhile, the guarantee of fixed indexed annuities is that *they never experience declines.* **The upside potential is a respectable near 6% annualized return, and losses are removed from the equation.**

Further, Dr. Ibbotson also argued that while fixed indexed annuities performed similarly to bonds up until 2016, this pattern is unlikely to continue: "It's pretty hard to have that today, when yields are below 3% on bonds." We understand this already, as this is due to our low interest rate environment (see Chapter 2).

Ibbotson concluded that fixed indexed annuities "have the potential to outperform bonds in the

Table 2: Simulated Investment Strategy Returns, 1927-2016

	Fixed Indexed Annuities	Long Term Government Bonds	Large Cap Stocks
Average Annual Return	5.81%	5.32%	9.92%
Minimum Annualized 3-Year Return	0.00%	-2.32%	-27.00%

Source: 2017 SSBI Yearbook, Roger G. Ibbotson

near future and smooth the return pattern of a portfolio, given the downside protection," making a strong case for fixed indexed annuities as a part of most retirement portfolios.

Rethink Recap: Rejecting "High Risk for High Returns"

Knowing what we know about fixed indexed annuities, how would we rewrite the saying, "No pain, no gain"? Maybe "No pain, still gains!" This is part of rethinking and challenging the taken-for-granted in retirement planning. It's more important than ever to reject the myth that returns require risk, and find an advisor who believes the same.

Chapter 5:
Instead of a Bucket, Have a Faucet

Main Ideas:

- One of the most common fears for retirees is longevity risk, or the risk that savings will run out.
- There are two ways to utilize your savings: as a bucket that you can draw from until it's empty, or as a faucet that keeps flowing.
- How can you create a faucet-like income stream to meet your life expenses?
- With your retirement advisor, you can find the right strategy for your retirement income needs.

A distraught senior called her doctor. "Is it true I have to take this new medication for the rest of my life?" she asked. "I'm afraid so" the doctor replied.

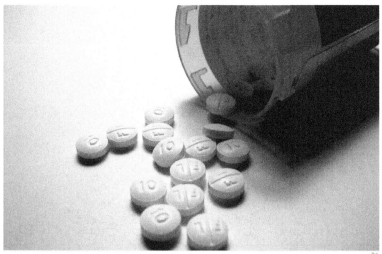

A prescription bottle, hopefully with refills. Photography by Tom Varco (2006).[26]

"Well," she said slowly, "I'm wondering if my condition is more serious than I thought. This prescription is marked 'no refills'!"

Does your retirement fund have "refills"? Which is better: the biggest shop-club-sized bottle of pills you can think of, that will *hopefully* last you for the rest of your life? Or a prescription bottle that you would recognize from your own medicine cabinet, *guaranteed* to have monthly refill privileges for life? Which do you trust to meet your needs?

In retirement, one of the biggest fears is longevity risk, or the danger that your life will last longer than your money. I find that regardless of how much money a client has, most are nervous that it is not enough. In a recent study with 3,000 individuals nearing retirement, 63% of seniors feared running out of money in retirement *more than they feared death.*[27] How can you ensure that your financial needs are met throughout your life?

Safety First

This type of retirement planning, meeting your essential needs above all else, is sometimes referred to as a "safety first" approach to retirement. Meaning, if your income needs are a certain amount per month, then you should have financial assets generating at least enough monthly income to provide for your expenses. These should be insulated from stock market gyrations, interest rate changes, and all those other anxieties that could keep you up at night. And here you thought income would end when you retired! It doesn't have to. **"Safety first" retirement planning emphasizes that regular, predictable income streams should continue in retirement to help you meet your financial obligations each and every month.**

One year, my son was a firefighter for Halloween. He loved thinking of himself as a safety hero. We had to practice saying, "Trick or treat!" because initially, all he wanted to say was hero catch phrases, like "Safety first!" I liked that this little guy was so committed to his role as a firefighter that he felt it was his duty to remind everyone to be safe. When I sit across from clients, I feel the same way in my fiduciary responsibility to put their interests and safety above all else.

So why is "safety first" planning so important? Because, unfortunately, savings can run out. Maybe not if you're extremely wealthy and have more money than you and your loved ones could spend in their lifetimes. That would be quite the "problem" to have! But just ask Gladys in the introduction of this book, and other seniors filing for bankruptcy, whose "bucket" of savings dried up prematurely. Instead, she needed a dependable faucet that will never stop flowing income for her.

One of my good friends from college has a great-grandfather that just celebrated his 105th birthday. He is happy, healthy, rarely uses his wheelchair, and enjoys spending time with his ten great-great-grandchildren. No financial advisor could have predicted that he'd be living off of his retirement plan for 40 years! He tells everyone that will listen about his elixir of life: guaranteed lifetime income from his annuities, paid every month. He knows he would not have been able to live comfortably on savings alone.

Income is More Important than Savings

While savings can run out, lifetime income is like that refillable prescription bottle that lasts as long as you do. As you approach retirement, it is critical to shift from building savings to creating a dependable monthly income stream. Talk with a retirement income planner and determine how to get the guaranteed lifetime income you need. For example, deferred fixed annuities, from Chapter 3, can deliver that stable, dependable income that your salary once did.

But what about easy access to all your money? Isn't it a quandary to tie up a portion of your savings, even if it is producing income? Retirement planning guru Stan Haithcock put it this way:

> There are the one-percenters who don't need an income [in retirement]... For the rest of us, the two questions we need to ask ourselves are, "How much risk am I willing to shoulder?" and "How much risk am I willing to transfer?" Annuities that contractually guarantee lifetime income are risk-transfer strategies. You are transferring the risk to the annuity carrier to pay you an income stream regardless of how long you live.[28]

Knowing that there will always be some amount of risk that you shoulder yourself, which risk are you willing to take?

The risk that you potentially could have made more money in the stock market?

or

The risk that your money might not last you for the remainder of your life?

By rethinking your retirement options and using those P-Rs of Safe Money (see page 29) as a guide, you can eliminate that longevity risk, while giving your money an opportunity to make competitive returns through products like fixed indexed annuities. But how much money do you need?

What's Your Retirement Number?

In some retirement planning commercials lately, we see individuals with dollar amounts, usually in the millions, floating by their heads or carried on their backs. A narrator invites us to use an online tool to discover our "retirement number." We are left with the impression that if we were to determine it, *that number* would be the amount we need to retire on our own terms and live comfortably for the remainder of our lives. Now, to be fair, marketers have a difficult task: retirement income planning involves complex analyses that no one could accurately depict in a short commercial. But the problem is that in making a memorable advertisement, it creates a cultural misunderstanding about saving for retirement.

Have you been thinking about the right number for you? According to a 2017 study by Wells Fargo and Gallup with over 1,000 investors, about half of those nearing retirement had a retirement number in mind. Most often, that number was $1 million.[29] Isn't it interesting that so many people with different life circumstances, health profiles, and family needs, all living in different parts of the country with varied costs of living, all still gave the same retirement number? How did they arrive at that figure?

A different survey from the Transamerica Center For Retirement Studies asked workers, "How did you determine how much money you'll need for retirement?" If you guessed, "They guessed it," you're right. Most said they went with a number they had read about or heard from somewhere, or just made up a number that sounded large enough.[30] Working towards retirement on a guess or a hunch is dangerous for several reasons.

First, most individuals struggle to determine the right number. It's difficult, especially when financial planning is not your expertise, to piece together a complete financial picture of your liabilities in retirement, such as taxes, long-term care estimations, Medicare drawdown stipulations, and other expenses. These are all factors an experienced advisor can help you better understand.

Second, even if you were to settle on a pile of money that you think would last your lifetime, the estimations may be off without your knowledge. This is like hiking through the woods to a destination without first checking that your compass accurately points due north! You may be confident and take pride in making strides towards your goal, but all the while, you're walking into the unknown with a false sense of security. All that confidence will seem sheepish if you learn that some minor adjustments along the way could have helped to reach your goals faster.

I met with a couple that estimated they needed $60,000 per year of retirement income, in addition to Social Security. Surprised, I probed, "Even in 10 years? While $60,000 could work next year, what about inflation? How much will it cost to buy $60,000 worth of goods and services in 10, 20, even 30 years?" Now it was their turn to be surprised. They hadn't factored inflation into their estimates, which would have compromised their buying power and lifestyle.

Third, retirement may change your habits and preferences in unexpected ways. I have learned that most people don't reduce their spending in retirement—if anything, they take that trip they always dreamed of, remodel their homes, and enjoy everything they couldn't do while stuck with a 9-to-5 job. "We call it deferred spending, or the 'Whee, I'm free' factor," says retiree Ellen Gerson of Florida. "We see all these folks retire and start doing all the things they were dying to do, from traveling to golfing to fixing up their houses. A year or two later, they look over their budgets and they've gone way over."[31]

If you're drawing from a large account, it may be tempting to think this large pile will last and last… until it's too late for you to change habits, perhaps go back into the workforce, or make adjustments to your retirement plan to prevent prematurely depleting your savings.

Good to Know: Inflation

Inflation is an increase in the price of goods and services in an economy over time. In the U.S., inflation is calculated through two measures:

1.) Consumer Price Index (CPI), which measures price changes for goods and services, from the perspective of the buyer. CPI looks at specific categories, like bread (a 66.5% increase just from 2000 to 2018!).

2.) Producer Price Indexes (PPI), which analyzes change over time in selling prices from the perspective of the seller.

The U.S. inflation rate has remained around 2-3% per year recently, with 2017 at 2.13% inflation. But, this is the national average. In fact, Phoenix had a reported 0.00% inflation rate in 2017. The highest two-year period of inflation in the past century was in 1979 (13.29%) and 1980 (12.52%).

Case Study:

Let's consider Ralph and Gloria, a couple in their early 90s in 2018, who retired at 65 in 1993. Prices have risen 74.7% since 1993, so they will need $1,747 to buy what they used to buy for $1,000 in 1993. If they needed $60,000 for living expenses in 1993, in 2018, they would need $104,819 to maintain that life-style.

Helpful calculators at: http://www.usinflationcalculator.com

Fourth, people nearing retirement may see that "retirement number" commercial featuring an actor with $1.5 million floating nearby and feel discouraged and panicked. It can be very hard for some to imagine a savings account with that much money available to pull from. "What if that's my number?" you might ask yourself. "Maybe it's better to not know." But, here's a secret: few people have $1.5 million in liquid assets. The trick is not to have that number in the bank upon retirement, *but to get that number*, in part through leveraging your savings for a guaranteed retirement income stream that will add up to that money you need over time.

A Gallup poll found that nearly all (98%!) non-retired investors "strongly agree" or "somewhat agree" that "it is important to have a guaranteed income stream in retirement, in addition to Social Security," and yet nearly half (49%) admitted that they are confused about how to get this additional income stream.[32] So, how do you get a guaranteed stream of income in retirement?

A Foundation of Income

Determining your income needs in retirement is similar to making a monthly budget. It requires you to take a look at the essentials, like housing, utilities, transportation, food, and other regular expenses, to determine how much income you need to pay your bills each month (with a little cushion for unexpected expenses, of course). Once you know what you need, you can piece together that amount of income through financial tools like:

- Social security
- Pensions
- 401(k) and IRAs
- Bond coupon payments
- Bank CDs
- Fixed annuities

Your qualified retirement advisor can work with you to find the appropriate sources of income to meet your expenses, with liquidity and growth opportunities. Added up, these create that "safety first" foundation of income. Once that is in place, then you can build in those extras, like trips or a home renovation that you are looking forward to in retirement.

Why is it important to calculate those income needs first? When building a house, or any building for that matter, the most important part is building the foundation. You want deep pilings, and level footings to carry the loads it will bear and resist anything nature will throw your way. If not, you'll have bigger problems down the road.

For generations, my extended family has lived in the San Francisco Bay area. I've been fascinated by a saga involving one of the city's downtown skyscrapers, Millennium Tower, a modern-day Titanic. Completed in 2008 for $350 million, it was by all accounts an impressive, state-of-the-art high-rise project. Like the Titanic, it also catered to the rich and famous, with over 400 lavish multimillion-dollar condo units occupied by celebrities and professional athletes. What else do the two have in common? Sinking.

By 2018, only 10 years after completion, the 58-story Millennium Tower had sunk 18 inches on one side and was leaning 14 inches northwest due to an improper foundational pillars in shifting soil

The sinking Millennium Tower, San Francisco, CA. Photo by Frank Schulenburg (2016).

conditions.[33] Engineers proposed drilling micro-pillars into the bedrock below the building, but the potential fix is estimated at up to $500 million—more than the original cost of the tower, and there's no guarantee it will work. And the building is not all that's sinking—the values of these luxury units have dropped considerably due to concerns that residents' safety is at stake.

I can't overstate the importance of a sure foundation. It is worth the time and effort to get it right and avoid the costly consequences. It may not be glamorous or flashy, and it's probably not what you close your eyes and dream of when you picture your retirement. It doesn't look like a cruise or a second home. But like Millennium Tower, those flashy dreams could be compromised if the foundation is not established first. The ground around us will always be shifting from economic woes, inflation, health concerns, and other issues. But you can have a sure foundation to help withstand those forces and give you peace of mind through it all.

Secure with Social Security?

Social Security, as we know it, is designed to be a source of lifetime income. Is this enough of a foundation? Your Social Security income amount is currently based on the highest 35 years of your work history, as well as the age when you begin distributions (a decision your retirement advisor can and should certainly weigh in on).

Despite the benefits, Social Security alone is not enough for most retirees. And that is true even if it remains at current funding levels, which we know is not likely. The Social Security Administration itself has a disclaimer *on your actual Social Security statement* that reads, "Congress has made changes to the law in the past and can do so at any time. The law governing benefit amounts may change because, by 2034, the payroll taxes collected will be enough to pay only about 79 percent of scheduled benefits."[34]

This ought to raise a red flag in all of our minds. Individuals in their 50s and 60s today will be right in the middle of their retirement years in 2034. Will

Congress act? *Yes, they have to.* Will they raise taxes and lower benefits? *Most likely.*

Pensions, as we discussed in Chapter 1, also can provide a part of the solution, and were designed to provide lifetime income to pensioners. Again, pensions provided certain assurances and guarantees that can help solve our two retirement planning needs: money to cover essential needs and money that lasts.

So, if you lack a pension, and Social Security is not enough, what options are available?

The Lifetime Income Annuity Solution

As I discussed in Chapters 3 and 4, one way to rethink your retirement is to use annuities—an insurance company product that protects your retirement assets and contractually provides a variety of benefits. When I talk to most clients, they tend to think of annuities in one way: a single deposit of money that gives the annuitant or owner a steady stream of income payments. What they are thinking of is a *lifetime immediate annuity.* These products are notorious for low returns, inflexibility, and non-existent beneficiary transfer, but the primary purpose was that stream of lifetime income payments. As I said in Chapter 3, these immediate annuities of the past have fallen out of favor; however, lifetime income—having a faucet instead of a bucket—is still an appealing idea.

Enter, the deferred fixed annuity with a *lifetime income rider*.

A *lifetime income rider* is a benefit that is attached to the same useful deferred fixed annuity product we've already discussed. With this additional rider, you can elect for a steady stream of payments that last a lifetime, either for just yourself, or to cover your spouse as well. These payments begin after a waiting period, hence the "deferred" annuity. Some deferrals can be as short as 30 days after your account is opened, others can be 10 years or longer. Like Social Security, payments tend to increase the longer you defer your income payments. And, these increases tend to be separate from the stock market, meaning, even if the market does not perform as expected, your future income level is guaranteed.

Why use a deferred fixed annuity instead of an immediate annuity? Easy—better benefits. While they may offer lifetime income, these are not your mother's annuities. Typical deferred fixed annuities with a *lifetime income rider* have the benefits you would expect from a deferred fixed annuity, like:

1. Account control and ability to withdraw your remaining value.
2. Beneficiary transfer options.
3. Guaranteed deferred income payout increases.

Immediate annuities tend to omit such benefits, focusing on lifetime income. A *deferred fixed annuity with a lifetime income rider* is a competitive product that offers the best of both an immediate lifetime annuity and a deferred fixed annuity.

In a *deferred fixed annuity with a lifetime income rider*, monthly income payments are guarantees written into the contract. Even though monthly lifetime income payments come from your annuity account balance, the insurance company is contractually bound to maintain these payments, even after the account balance has gone to zero.

As long as you live, there is no end to that faucet of steady income. The account may not be able to have a lump sum withdrawal or beneficiary transfer at this point; but, each reliable income payment will be like a support pillar, meeting your foundational needs for the rest of your life, just as they are for my friend's 105 year-old great-grandfather.

Why are lifetime income riders such a key component to your retirement portfolio? No matter what twists and turns, in life or in the economy, it is money you can never outlive, not to mention an added bonus of much more flexibility and liquidity than pensions or immediate annuities of yesteryear.

Good to Know: Insurance Riders

Insurance policies, be it life insurance, automobile insurance, or home insurance, usually have available features or benefits that can be added to them, called "riders." For example, in a homeowners' insurance policy, you may have a unique and valuable item that you wanted covered, that might be above and beyond typical coverage. In this case, you may want to look into a special "rider," or a protection guarantee, to add to your policy to cover the item.

Annuities, like other insurance products, allow riders so that you can customize the policy for you and offer you an additional guarantee, sometimes included in the policy, and sometimes added for a small fee. It's like extra insurance within your insurance. Some of these riders might be:

- Guaranteed increases to your income payout as you defer your income payments. These increases are insulated from the stock market and have guaranteed income growth.
- Impaired risk or terminal illness riders, where your entire annuity value can be accessed early in case of an accident or life-threatening disease.
- Nursing home, or long-term care riders, where a monthly income for payment doubles when you provide proof that the owner or annuitant has entered a nursing facility.
- Cost of living, or inflation-adjusted rider, which involves increasing monthly income payouts over time to combat inflation.

Renowned economist Dr. Wade Pfau has published "Six Habits of Naïve Investors." One of the main bad habits? He says naïve investors ignore and misunderstand annuities.[35] To break this habit, he suggests that investors need to "view annuities as insurance against outliving one's wealth" and provide "guaranteed income for life." With rising retirees' bankruptcy filings, we need that type of insurance. He suggests that retirees put part of their savings in a lifetime income annuity, while another part continues to grow in the stock market. Sound familiar? These are the basic tenets of the Rule of 100!

The Drawbacks of Drawdown Schedules

Speaking of the stock market, what about "drawdown schedules"? Wall Street advisors tend to discuss retirement planning quite differently. They typically suggest that their clients plan to take their lump sum of retirement assets and advocate a "safe" withdrawal rate of 4-5% per year to meet living expenses. This assumes quite a lot. Let's break down some of those assumptions:

- *Account has gains each year that allow retirees to pull from gains or interest instead of principal.* In order for funds to not dry up prematurely, it's key to leave as much as possible of the principal intact. What about economic slowdowns or downturns? Since Wall Street lacks principal protection, a severe market correction can hurt retirees' principal, the very thing that the 4% drawdown is based on. It's simply too much to ask for someone on a fixed income to not take a withdrawal one year due to a market crash.

- *Investors are disciplined enough to draw down only 4-5%.* When retirees were asked how much they anticipated needing to withdraw from their retirement portfolio each year, 81% estimated needing an average of 7%.[36] Remember that the principal needs to stay in place as much as possible. With a 7% drawdown, the principal will erode. Even with modest growth, the entire balance could be gone in less than 20 years. This is not long enough for many people, leaving retirees most vulnerable at the end of their lives when they need income most.

- *Account growth will outpace inflation.* This may be difficult to do in conservative, or low-return, models, especially if the advisor is charging high management fees.

- *Even in a best-case scenario, 4-5 percent may not be enough to last.* Wells Fargo Asset Management warned in 2017 that even well-positioned retirees who are disciplined to take only 5% maximum **still run a 20–30% risk of running out of money in retirement.** This is coming from Wall Street asset management advisors—they recognize their own products carry substantial risks.

Drawdown schedules might be right for some retirees, but for others, they are better avoided. Let's think again about that big-box, shop-club pill bottle tactic. Is one large bottle, carefully siphoned over time, going to last you the rest of your life? Isn't it better to meet with a professional that can look at your needs and write a prescription policy for lifetime unlimited refills?

A "safety first" tactic uses all available sources, like Social Security and deferred fixed annuities with lifetime income riders, to create an ample, refillable stream of retirement funds that meets your monthly and yearly needs.

Fitting it All In

So what should I do about Wall Street funds?
When is a drawdown schedule appropriate?
What about the Rule of 100?

When foundational income planning comes from the safe money side of your Rule of 100 allocation, you can feel more comfortable that you have your essential needs met *without question*. That's the peace-of-mind that quiets those anxieties that keep you up at night. Once that is in place, you and your advisor certainly can use the Rule of 100 to allocate what remains into the stock market. Remember: safety is best, then invest the rest. Since these funds are not needed for immediate income, you can ride out the ups and downs of the stock market without stressing about the day-to-day. You can enjoy historically strong long-term returns without worrying about your short-term needs.

Because when it all boils down, the best feature of the Rule of 100 is that your money is divided up to serve unique, complementary functions for your retirement plan. One part of your money meets your income needs and is protected from loss. Another part of your money continues to grow, and can benefit you and your heirs in the future.

Rethink Recap: And They Lived Happily Ever After

Remember the University of Michigan study cited in Chapter 1 that found that those with pensions are the happiest retirees?[37] You're in luck, because the study found that their happiness was tied with one other group: **those with** *deferred fixed annuities with lifetime income*. This makes sense, because with dependable "mailbox money" for life, from either a pension or an annuity, you avoid those gripping fears of longevity risk and instead enjoy peace-of-mind. You won't rattle that proverbial pill bottle and wonder if you're going to run out, because you know you are entitled to unlimited refills for life, like a faucet that will never run dry. If you were thinking that dependable income was limited to those with pensions, think again! Rethink guaranteed income and the impact a lifetime income annuity rider could have on your well-being in retirement.

Conclusion

Albert Einstein once humbly claimed, "I have no special talents. I am only passionately curious." I know I fall far short of Einstein-level brilliance. But questioning things? That's a quality that I think all of us can tap into. After all, the root of "question" is "quest." Curiosity begins that quest to find valuable information.

In my career, I field questions every day. I enjoy hearing about what people are curious about. But I find some of these questions are motivated less by passion, and more by a gloomy cloud of anxiety and guilt. Questions like:

Should I have saved more up to this point?
Will I lose my home?
What if I don't have enough money each year?
Will I become a burden on my children?

Where do these questions come from? Longevity risk concerns. Especially in this age of unprecedented bankruptcy filings for seniors, longevity anxiety seems to also be at an all-time high. Clients from every financial situation, every walk of life, and every type of career express these common fears.

When I talk with worried clients, I tell them two things:

1. No one knows how many years to count on. On the Actuaries Longevity Illustrator website (www.longevityillustrator.org), you can enter basic demographic information, like your age and gender, as well as your health status, to get an estimate of your chances of living to a certain age. But this is just what actuaries predict for people who share your characteristics.

2. Because of life expectancy unknowns, the exact answers to these questions are unknown. No prediction can offer you a definite answer for your own future, so stewing over it is unproductive—even counterproductive if it makes you worried sick! What proactive strategies could you and your advisor be taking instead?

The Right Answers to the Right Questions

In this emphasis on rethinking and reconsidering all worthwhile options to prepare for retirement, I've asked several questions so far. These useful questions to consider in your own retirement preparations include:

How much of your savings is at risk in Wall Street?
Is your account allocated based on the Rule of 100?
Do you have bonds, or bond funds instead?
What have you heard about annuities, and from what source?
What are your monthly retirement income needs?

But what about your questions? I'm sure at this point, there are several things on your mind, like:
How could this information work for me?
I'm not retiring until ____. How do I prepare now?
What would be right for my unique family situation?
Now what?

What Are You Playing At?

Each financial option, from pensions to 401(k)s, Wall Street equities to bonds, fixed annuities to fixed indexed annuities, are like a piece of the retirement income puzzle, and together can complete your retirement picture. But unlike a traditional puzzle, that picture on the box varies for each person. That's why asking the right kind of questions is important, because it helps you and your advisor determine what you need (see Appendix for a list of helpful questions to ask, including the questions above and more). For most, the ideal retirement picture ensures you have enough to cover your living essentials and maintain your desired quality of life, or "safety first" planning (see Chapter 5). For some, the picture includes additional features, such as legacy planning and passing on as much as possible to heirs.

It's easy, even for some financial advisors, to focus on maximizing gains and minimizing losses as the end goal. Even I get caught up into wanting to maximize my clients ROI or "Return on Investment." In my years as a financial advisor, I acquired an art print from the Museum of American Finance in New York City. It's a reproduction of an 1883 board game, "Bulls and Bears: The Great Stock Market Game." Historian Margaret K. Hofer said, *"The financial panic of 1873, the worst before 1929, inspired this board game, in which the Bulls and the Bears (the speculators) are depicted fleecing the sheep (the public)."*

The cover of an 1883 McLoughlin Bros. board game, depicting Wall Street as a cut-throat game.

I keep the print in my office as a reminder that there are shrewd players who get so caught up in the "game" and trying to "win" that they can lose sight of what really matters.

Because when it comes down to it, it shouldn't be a game of chance—it ought to a puzzle. There should be no risky moves to gain a lead, no concept of winners and losers, just methodical client-centered planning at your pace to complete your personal retirement picture. It may even include things that can't simply be quantified, like the peace of mind of guaranteed lifetime income. A qualified retirement advisor listens to you describe your personal retirement picture, identifies how components could work together, and works piece by piece to make that picture a reality.

Now is the Time

Speaking of a game of chance, the data on Wall Street truly speaks for itself. While the stock market is unpredictable, there is a real possibility that you and your retirement fund will live through two or more major stock market corrections, since they tend to happen once a decade, on average.

Are you ready? Now is the time to:

- *Use advanced financial tools that debunk the risk for returns myth and offer the P-Rs of Safe Money (see page 29).*

- *Leverage your current money to create a future income stream, a vital need 98% of Americans agree on.*

- *Plan ahead for your retirement with a qualified advisor, protecting a portion of your savings from loss, inflation, and fees.*

Talk About Passionate Curiosity

How can someone develop passionate curiosity about retirement? It's easier than you think, and you're probably well on your way.

1. **Self-talk.** Tell yourself that you are already on the right track. You've taken an active interest in your retirement just by reading through this guide. Remember, just as you likely trained for your decades-long career with education or vocational training, you are now educating yourself for a decades-long retirement. Both life phases take curiosity and level-headed preparation, and you should feel proud of your efforts.

2. **Talk to loved ones.** What are the financial priorities for you and your family? This is what you've worked and saved for—now what do you plan to do? A combination of savings and retirement income is likely key. The truth is that our economy hasn't ever ushered seniors into retirement with 401(k)s before. Without pensions providing monthly income, it's more important than ever to use careful planning.

3. **Talk to others** about their retirement plans. You are part of the first 401(k) generation, which means you are preparing for retirement differently than any generation that has come before. You're not alone, and you might find other folks are working through similar questions and concerns.

4. **Talk to a retirement advisor.** It's very understandable to put this off, unsure about what you'll hear. But remember—what you don't know *can* hurt you. When it comes time to shift the majority of your portfolio to safety, do it with your eyes wide open, partnered with someone whose expertise is in safe, income-generating planning. It's too important to not use the best options available.

Let's think about that Einstein quote one more time: "I have no special talents. I am only passionately curious." There's no substitute for taking the time to ask questions and find solutions. Talent and brilliance won't do it all, because ultimately it comes down to interest and effort to get us there. Imagine a future conversation with a friend:

Friend: *"You seem like you're really enjoying retirement. What's your secret?"*

You: *"No special talents, really. I was just curious about what I could do to improve retirement, so I found a retirement advisor who could help me. We had an honest*

> *conversation about my questions and goals, then I studied the options and found a plan that works for me."*

This doesn't have to be just an imagined future. It's one that I've seen individuals achieve from all walks of life. Today, I invite you to get closer to living out the reality that you imagine for yourself. When it comes to retirement, don't just think about it—rethink about it.

Disclaimers

Nathan Frederico is the President of Mayfield Financial Group, Inc. Information contained in this text and any recommended websites or other materials are for informational purposes only. They should not be considered legal, tax, investment or financial advice. You should also consult with a licensed financial advisor before making any financial or retirement decisions. You should consult with an attorney to determine what is best for your legal needs. As such, you should consult with a licensed tax professional, such as a Certified Public Accountant or Enrolled Agent, to determine what is best for your tax needs.

The author does not make any guarantee or other promise as to any results that may be obtained from using this book's content. No one should make any financial or retirement decisions without first consulting their financial advisor and conducting their own research and due diligence. To the maximum extent permitted by law, the author disclaims any and all liability in the event any commentary, analysis, information, opinions, advice, and/or recommendations prove to be inaccurate, outdated, incomplete, unreliable, and/or result in any financial or other losses.

No advisor-client or attorney-client relationship is formed through requesting, receiving, or reading this book.

Your use of the information in this text or the linked websites is at your own risk, and should be done while counseling with qualified professionals as to their suitability to your individual needs.

References

[1] Thorne, Deborah, Pamela Foohey, Robert M. Lawless, and Katherine M. Porter. 2018, August 5. "Graying of U.S. Bankruptcy: Fallout from Life in a Risk Society." Indiana Legal Studies Research Paper, No. 406.

[2] Paine, Alfred Bigelow. (2016). Mark Twain, A Biography, 1835-1910, The Personal and Literary Life of Samuel Langhorn Clemens. *Project Gutenberg EBook.*

[3] Ortiz, Jorge L. (2018, June 11). "In baseball, numbers are everything. Why 10 matters to most MLB veterans." *USA Today.* http://www.usatoday.com/story/sports/mlb. /2018/06/11/mlb-10-years-service-time-benefits-pension/682546002/

[4] Clements, Jonathan. 2005, July 27. "The Secret to a Happy Retirement: Friends, Neighbors, and a Fixed Annuity." *Wall Street Journal.* http://online.wsj.com/ad/article/jh_secret_happy_retirement

[5] Stanford Center on Longevity. 2014. http://longevity.stanford.edu/

[6] Morrissey, Monique. 2016, March 3. "The State of American Retirement: How 401(k)s Have Failed Most Americans." *Economic Policy Institute.*

[7] Graves, Will. 2017, March 28. "Pension Acts: An Overview of Revolutionary War Pension and Bounty Land Legislation." http://revwarapps.org/revwar-pension-acts

[8] Beard, Mary. *SPQR: A History of Ancient Rome.* New York: Liveright.

[9] Holland, Kelley. 2015, March 23. "For millions, 401(k) plans have fallen short." *CNBC.* https://www.cnbc.com/2015/03/20/l-it-the-401k-is-a-failure.html

[10] Staff. 1984, December 3. "President Reagan on Pensions." *Employee Benefit Research Institute.* https://www.ebri.org/pdf/notespdf/11-1284notes.pdf

[11] Pew Charitable Trusts. 2017, January. "Small Business Views on Retirement Savings Plans." *Pew Charitable Trusts* http://www.pewtrusts.org/~/media/assets/2017. /01/small-business-survey-retirement-savings_f.pdf

[12] Vanguard. 2017. "How America Saves 2017." *Nerd Wallet* https://www.nerdwallet. com/article/the-average-retirement-savings-by-age-and-why-you-need-more

[13] Ghilarducci, Theresa and Wei Sun. 2006. "How defined contribution plans and 401(k)s affect employer pension costs." *Journal of Pension Economics and Finance,* 5(2), 175-96.

[14] Olshan, Jeremey. 2011, November 22. "'Father' of the 401(k)'s Tough Love." *Marketwatch.* http://blogs.marketwatch.com/encore/2011/11/22/father-of-the-401ks-tough-love/.

[15] Martin, Timothy W. 2017, January 2. "The Champions of the 401(k) Lament the Revolution they Started." *Wall Street Journal.* https://www.wsj.com/articles/the-champions-of-the-401-k-lament-the-revolution-they-started-1483382348.

[16] Vernon, Stephen. 2016, October 16. "A Retirement Income Strategy for Do-It-Yourselfers." *CBS News.* https://www.cbsnews.com/news/a-retirement-income-strategy-for-do-it-yourselfers/.

[17] Bogle, John. 2010. *Common Sense on Mutual Funds,* pg. 87-88. New York: Wiley.

[18] Schwartz, Shelley. 2014, April 10. "Bonds vs. Bond Funds: What You Need to Know Now." *CNBC.* https://www.cnbc.com/2014/04/10/bonds-vs-bond-funds-what-you-need-to-know-now.html.

[19] Brown, Joshua. 2005, March 25. "The Biggest Mistake Investors are Making Right Now." http://fortune.com/2015/03/25/unconstrained-bond-funds-risk

[20] Konisberg, Ruth Davis. 2014, October 20. "Why I Won't Own Bond Funds in My Retirement Portfolio." *Time*. http://time.com/money/3524487/retirement-bond-funds-avoid/

[21] Lake, Rebecca. 2017, February 7. "Fixed Annuities Versus Bonds: Which is Better for Retirement?" *U.S. News*. https://money.usnews.com/investing/articles/2017-02-07/fixed-annuities-versus-bonds-which-is-better-for-retirement

[22] Scheer, Stefan. 2007. "Magic Mountain in Corkscrew at Gardaland, Italy." https://en.wikipedia.org/wiki/File:MagicMountain_Gardaland_Screw.jpg

[23] Sinclair, Upton. 1994 [1934]. *I, Candidate for Governor, and How I Got Licked*. Berkeley, CA: University of California Press.

[24] Kahneman, Daniel and Amos Tversky. 1979. "Prospect Theory: An Analysis of Decision Under Risk." *Econometrica* 47(2): 263-91.

[25] Britton, Diana. "2018, March 7. "Ibbotson: Fixed Indexed Annuities Beat out Bonds." https://www.wealthmanagement.com/insurance/ibbotson-fixed-indexed-annuities-beat-out-bonds

[26] Vacro, Tom. 2006. "Escitalopram 10mg Tablets" https://commons.wikimedia.org/wiki/File:Lexapro_pills.jpg

[27] Allianz Life. 2017, September 21. *2017 Generations Ahead Study*

[28] Haithcock, Stan. 2016, October 18. "Do You Hate Annuities? Here's Why You Might Want to Change Your Mind." *The Street*. http://www.thestreet.com/story/13855335/1/do-you-hate-annuities-here-s-why-you-might-want-to-change-your-mind.html

[29] Wells Fargo Institutional Retirement. 2017. "2017 Wells Fargo retirement study." https://www.wellsfargo.com/com/retirement-employee-benefits/retirement/perspectives/

[30] Collinson, Catherine. 2015. "Retirement throughout the ages: An examination of preparations and expectations among American workers." https://www.transamericacenter.org/docs/default-source/resources/center-research/16th-annual/tcrs2015_wp_retirement_throughout_the_ages.pdf

[31] Haiken, Melanie. "10 Biggest Retirement Mistakes—And How to Avoid Them." https://www.gilbertguide.com/retirement-mistakes.

[32] Saad, Lydia. 2018, January 2. "Investors want Freedom with Retirement Savings." *Gallup*.https://news.gallup.com/poll/225023/investors-no-strings-attached-retirement-income-stream.aspx.

[33] Robinson, Melia. 2018, July 24. "A 58-story skyscraper in San Francisco is tilting and sinking — and residents say their multimillion-dollar condos are 'nearly worthless'" *Business Insider* https://www.businessinsider.com/is-millennium-tower-safe-still-leaning-sinking-2017-9

[34] Social Security Administration. 2018. "Your Social Security Statement."

[35] Pfau, Wade. 2106, May 5. "The Value of Sound Financial Decisions: From Alpha to Gamma." *Forbes*. https://www.forbes.com/sites/wadepfau/2016/05/05/the-value-of-sound-financial-decisions-from-alpha-to-gamma/#7be0275b55df

[36] Saad, Lydia. 2018, January 2. "Investors want Freedom with Retirement Savings." *Gallup*.https://news.gallup.com/poll/225023/investors-no-strings-attached-retirement-income-stream.aspx.

[37] Clements, Jonathan. 2005, July 27. "The Secret to a Happy Retirement: Friends, Neighbors, and a Fixed Annuity" *Wall Street Journal*.

About the Author

Nathan R. Frederico, Certified Financial Fiduciary® and Retirement Income Certified Professional® is the host of the *Worry-free Financial Solutions* radio program and podcast, offering timely advice to thousands of current and pre-retirees who want to improve their financial peace of mind in retirement. As president of Mayfield Financial Group, he offers a safety-first approach to retirement planning.

Nathan received a Bachelor of Science degree in Economics from Brigham Young University in Utah, where he studied finance and market trends. He began a decade-long career as an investment analyst and portfolio manager. His dissatisfaction with the industry's insatiable appetite for risk led him to rethink approaches for stable, competitive returns. He found his passion at Mayfield Financial, as he helps clients minimize risk while achieving their retirement and financial goals.

Nathan enjoys living in Tucson, Arizona with his wife and their children.

Made in the USA
Las Vegas, NV
02 July 2021